EVERYTHING EXCEPT CORN PASTA

---a culinary guide for backpackers

I0164728

By Carol Wellman

This cookbook is dedicated to David "Rainmaker" Mauldin who has helped me test many unusual recipes and shared many culinary adventures. My goal is to entertain you with stories and offer recipes that might acquaint you with the sensory luxuries and deprivations possible while pursuing a long trail.

May the trailgods gift you with treasures useful in this art, along with any others they deem interesting.

I don't have any degrees in culinary or medical fields. Follow all advice and suggestions at your own risk. --Carol "Brawny" Wellman

No, I Absolutely did Not drink your beer !

All hikers know the two second rule....or was it three seconds? Any food that drops on the ground is fair game after three seconds, max. I'm not sure about beer left to chill in a creek.

All rights reserved. Written and illustrated by Carol Wellman. No portion may be reproduced without written consent of author. All sketches are copy writed by Carol Wellman.

A Fire Creek Pass Publication
First Edition June 30, 2011
Second Edition October 20, 2013

ISBN 0-9728154-3-0

A hiker hikes on his feet.
A hiker hikes on his wallet.
A hiker hikes on his stomach.

These first lines I wrote years ago. I still believe all of these statements are valid, and while this collection of recipes and true stories may not deal much with the first statement, it is my intention to lessen the blow on second and make the third simply say, "General, the troops are ready and willing."

You're probably thinking, "What? Troops? Hiking on my stomach? What **is** she talking about? Well, let's get started and head out on this adventure together.

Among the ranks of long distance hikers you will find a great deal of diversity in the amount of time, money and energy devoted to amassing food supplies. While some are totally health food oriented, no additives or preservatives please, some going so far as to sprout seeds en route, others will download anything not claimed or watched, whether it is in town or trail. This last I understand.

The worst hunger I ever experienced in my life was when we were sitting on a narrow ledge on the Pacific Crest Trail eating lunch. I had finished my allotment for that meal break. There were still two long days of steady hiking until we reached town and could resupply. I measured my food carefully, each meal rationing the predetermined amount, regardless. And today was no different, but, after I finished lunch, I felt like I was really starving.

Rainmaker was still relaxing in the shade. I had time to kill. I looked at my pack, trying to remember anything surplus or edible tucked inside, anything I could eat right now. Vitamins. A tad of peanut butter. Well, I thought, considering the scanty food bag, I probably wouldn't need breakfast the last day on the trail. Suddenly, I remembered the scraps left from my Glorified Cold Cereal. I drug that out. Scarfed it down, drank a pint of water and licked my lips, wondering, "What else is there? A bit of cheese?" I thought of my toothpaste.

I paused, heard female voices drifting up the trail and the steady clip clop of heavy animals. I gazed down the trail, searching for the cause of these rare sounds. At last I saw them. It was some horse women trudging up the trail, holding the reigns of their animals. They were getting closer. I had to move. In the effort to stay on the edge of the mountain and still let the women and their four horses pass by, my eating frenzy stopped while I scooted back behind a cliff hanging tree.

Their arrival was a blessing in disguise. Moral of story, if you believe in morals, is never under estimate hiker hunger. Always bring enough, an extra day's food at the least, preferably something you can stand. It is my sincere hope that this cookbook will provide you with plenty of ideas and recipes for food that you can stand. Sometimes the food suggestions seem bizarre. One critic said it was obvious a real hiker never wrote these recipes. No real long distance hiker would eat or cook like this.

Let me assure you I have and I did. After five months on the trail, food takes on new meaning. The poptart that used to make your mouth salivate now causes nausea. Rainmaker used to swear by poptarts smeared with chunky style peanut butter. After two months of backpacking, mention of either brought icy stares of revulsion.

It is good to journey towards an end
But in the end.
Its all about the food.

I created this pen and ink sketch after thru hiking the Appalachian Trail. After cresting a rock outcropping, I turned around and saw Hoosier coming over the hill. I took his photo. Later, I was inspired to add the saying "It is good to journey towards an end, but in the end it's all about the food."

As an extremist and die-hard Ultralighter, I actually break some of my own safety rules on occasion by cooking a meager meal before bed then hiking into town completely empty. I talk about that extreme behavior in the chapter called **Special Tricks for Ultralighters**. I try to never go empty unless I'm positive of where I am. The hunger spurs me to hike faster and the temporary discomfort lasts a few hours. Meanwhile I am dreaming of the things I am going to eat first.

Most don't want to hike hungry, ever, which is very normal. Hopefully these pages will inspire you to scope out new foods, slowly walk the aisles in your local grocery, rather than ordering another Mountain House meal. I'm sure most of us agree that the journey is good if the food was great.

Some of the tools that will come in handy as you prepare the recipes found in this book are:

rolling pin
cutting board
sharp knifes
microwavable bowls in several sizes
dehydrator, with sauce trays
hand held mixer, or blender, or both
measuring cups
measuring spoons
Ziploc bags, in various sizes
non-stick pan spray
baking pans, square, 9x13, cookie sheet with sides
spray bottle, to which you'll add one drop chlorine per liter bottle(for prepping fruits and vegetables)
various plastic containers with lids for long term storage

TABLE OF CONTENTS

Forward

First, let me extend a special thanks to all my trail friends who showed me various methods of dealing with food.

The famous Gorp mixtures that actually increased in volume as we made our way up the trail, often taking on leftovers from the hiker box found in the corner of the Trail Town's tiny Post Office, were so memorable. Who knew you could put candy corn and freeze dried peas along with honey mustard pretzels in the same gallon Ziploc bag? Then, the couple who admitted to buying fifty-two candy bars and two packs of ramen noodles in Stehekin as their last resupply made me rethink the food pyramid theory completely. I mean, if there is enough protein and carbs, who cares if you're getting any vitamin B?

Then, I'd follow The Berry Eaters who casually stripped every edible from bushes without missing a step. They had that down. If the thimble berries or wild blueberries reappeared, you knew that hiker was in town, or slept in, letting you get ahead.
There hikers who knew every tavern within half a mile of a road crossing, seeking hot food and a beer at the pub. When they joined you in the shelter, you'd find out what you missed by trekking north across that road, instead of going east two tenths of a mile where the grilled burgers made your mouth water and the beer was ice cold.

And no disrespect intended, but there are always those who swear by the prepackaged meals, Mountain House advocates. And it was true. The nutritional information promised that after eating such a meal, which you could conveniently cook in its own pouch, you would have provided your body with at least 100% of all the vitamins and minerals you needed.

For weeks, I watched in awe as Smurf would rise with the dawn, shiver and stand cooking oatmeal at the picnic table, his feet stomping along frosted grass ways. Meanwhile, I hunkered down in the 30 degree-goose down, sleeping bag. The oatmeal would taste good, but I am a Two-Pop Tarts on the move kind of gal. Throw everything into the pack on those cold mornings, put on gloves, shoulder the pack, grab my poles and go, chomping on the poptarts while hiking that first mile of many. By the time breakfast was eaten, I was warmed up, smiling at the new buds on the wild roses.

I learned how to find and harvest wild onions on the PCT, nearing Vermillion Valley. Turns out, wild onions added to ramen noodles are pretty decent. Nettles, I found will add volume and lose their prickliness when cooked. My dreams were more vivid when eating those nettles. I often wondered if there is something to that?

Of course, the Three Second Rule became really important. If something dropped on the ground and the owner made no move to reclaim it, it is fair game. A couple times it came down to one or two m&ms. Blow on them and they are considered clean.

One day I hiked with a guy growing his own sprouts in a plastic jar. Twice a day he would rinse the seeds. The sun did its work, he said, and they never got moldy. I found it an interesting concept, but never actually tried it.

I met a big tall guy who carried a small can of pineapple for each day on the trail. He said the weight didn't bother him. He just loved pineapple enough to do it. I asked about the cans. He said, "So they weigh a little, no deal." He claimed he packed the empties out, leaving no trace. I believed him, too.

Allow me too, to express much appreciation to all the trail angles who supplemented our meager food bags along the way. Those treats of peanut brittle and root beer stashed in trail coolers tasted mighty fine. And to the trail maintainer who left a canister of fresh homemade brownies in the shelter in Massachusetts, I send a huge God Bless you.

If you read this book and recognize the special part you have played, thank you, and please remember the million smiles you brought to all of us who were out there on some sort of Journey, for better or worse.

May all your trails be lighter.

Saving fuel but still having it hot is really an art form.

There are many different types of backpacking stoves. Some are much quicker than others, bringing things to a rapid boil in mere minutes, while some are able to simmer on half an ounce of fuel. One thing common among hikers, though, is the desire to save fuel both for economy and weight.

Imagine you have just finished cooking your supper, and something unexpected comes up, like a nature call or furry visitor. Perhaps you have thought of something to write in your journal, or want to put on more clothes against the night chill. At this point, you can take immediate action to keep your food warm, if not hot, for four to five minutes without having to reheat it.

Primarily, you must insulate your pot. If you still have some heat at the bottom and there isn't any flame, do not remove the pot, but insulate it from the sides and especially on top. This may be done by wrapping your windscreen and then your camp towel around the sides. On top place some small article of clothing, like mittens, bandana or hat. You can use your hiking boot as a cup holder to keep coffee hot longer. The cup will be insulated by the boot on all sides except the top. Cover the cup, and the coffee will stay hot even longer.

A very valuable item I made and field tested is the Pot Cozy, an insulated foam nest made to snug around your own special pot and lid. Directions for making one are given in Everything Except. You can make this pot cozy with the trimmed off length of a closed cell sleeping pad.

Hot salsa is risky on the trail.

While rummaging through a hiker box, I found some free individual packages of salsa. I smiled, imagining how great it would taste with my rather bland store brand corn tortillas. But that night, sitting beside my tent, liberally smearing it on my supper tortillas, I wished I had another quart of water. One bite told me it was way too hot for my liking. If this happens to you, your supper can be a painful reminder how important water is. You may not have enough water with you to alleviate the ensuing pain.

My method of keeping things cold, at least for a little while.

Most areas of the country cool off considerably at night, especially the desert and high country. Use this fact to your advantage. If you have cheese and soft breads with you, they will keep much longer if allowed to cool at night, outside the pack. In the morning, wrap the chilled items in clothing and store them deep in your pack. At lunch or supper, pull out the item, break off a chunk and immediately return to it's place deep in the pack. Repeat this strategy all week as needed.

Pure chocolate candy bars are very hard to eat if they get warm and melt. What a mess! Choose candy that can take the heat if you're going through the desert in July, or the cornfield in Pennsylvania. M&Ms do great, as do unfrosted granola bars and hard candy. Snicker's bars are a favorite, but they get so smeary if left in the sun you have to lick the wrapper.

Don't mix things that must be cooked with things that can be eaten raw.
Ramen noodles are great eaten straight out of the package, uncooked. Quick cooking raw oatmeal can be eaten this way, as well as cheeses and jerky. I discovered that these make great emergency foods because they do not require time or fuel to cook them.

However, as I learned trailside, if you mix them in Ziploc bags with cooking-required-for-digestion foods they become less available. For instance, angel hair spaghetti cooks fine in about 5 minutes, but it's very hard to eat raw. Once, running short on lunches, I realized I had plenty of mixed pastas. Unhappily, I had mixed ramen and angle hair. I was reduced to picking the edible ramen noodles out of my supper mix. Raw *quick cooking* oats can be eaten straight. Steel cut oats require more water and fuel for cooking and don't digest as well. Cheese and jerky can be eaten alone. If these are mixed with macaroni or dehydrated vegetables in a bag, they aren't very accessible as snacks on the go.

Most breads and cookies make great crumbs.

Be prepared to eat cookies, pastry and corn tortillas with a spoon. In the first couple days of a long section, you can spread these items with peanut butter because they are probably still in large pieces. If they turn to crumbs, they may be used with your cold breakfast cereals or stirred together with peanut butter and shaped into balls.

Powders, such as coffee and dry milk, escape no matter what.

A designated "powders bag" is essential to keeping everything under control. Use one large Ziploc bag to hold all the small Ziploc bags of various powders. Somehow, no matter how new or brand name the plastic bag is, powders will escape, that's why I double the bag whenever possible. Remember to label each bag. Sugar and salt can look similar. A hiker once tasted some white powder to find out whether it was laundry soap or dry milk. It was laundry soap.

Get the best Ziploc bags you can find.

A Ziploc bag that won't hold a seal, or tears at the top when you use it is not worth much. Buy good ones, the best you can find, and they will last you for several hundred miles. Poor quality bags will cause you hours of discontent and cursing when foods escape into stuff sacks or cold fingers cannot negotiate a successful seal.

Sometimes dumpster diving isn't all it's cracked up to be.

Always test your gear before leaving on a long journey.

It's wise to test your new recipes when you're at home and can throw it away and eat something else. Hiker boxes abound with the same trail mixtures. It's like the same recipe was shipped in from different states by people who had read the same books.

Apparently these foods were made in bulk, portioned into baggies and shipped via drop boxes. But, nearly all backpackers find they tire of even their favorite foods after weeks of eating the same things. Prepacked drop boxes of these same foods end up getting left stop after stop. Variety is the spice of life, trail food included.

Hiking partners might want to cook separately. It works.

It may seem unusual for committed partners to cook separately. It worked for Rainmaker and me because we had different methods and evening routines.

In town we each bought and carried out what we enjoyed eating. We could gauge our weights and satisfy food cravings individually. Sometimes his experiences caused him to choose things I would never have thought of, like wheat tortillas. Once, thinking to outdo him, I bought corn tortillas. Mistake, but at least I was the one to suffer the consequences. Not once was there an argument over food choices, who ate what, or when.

I liked coffee first thing, after pitching our evening camp. Rain would have his with dessert. I never presoaked food. Rainmaker always did. In the early days, we each carried Esbit stoves with hexamine tablets for fuel. When, the soda can stove, sometimes called the Pepsi can stove, replaced the esbit stove, we were able to easily adapt in our own ways. This ultra-light method of solo cooking allows the either partner to continue the hike if one chooses to leave the trail. If the partners split each still has cookware to continue separately.

Never use dried beans or split peas in instant cooking concoctions.

We found a bag of peas, seeds and rice in a baggie, along with various spices, donated to a hiker box. Rainmaker picked it up, threw it in his pack. The resort town along the PCT was expensive and had little to offer. But, two nights later, he discovered that no amount of cooking would soften the split peas. Bottom line, it was a waste of fuel, food and valuable daylight. IN the end, he had no supper and a growling stomach. I offered him something, but he refused. If you want to bring peas or seeds because of the proteins and enzymes, always grind any uncooked beans to a fine powder before adding to a recipe. Or, if you prefer, cook until very tender, then dehydrate.

My 3-ounce cook set from the Appalachian Trail. Notice the soda can stove, pot support and aluminum lid. All of this nests inside the plastic container used for coffee and rehydrating foods.

Every hiker needs one good spoon.

You can eat anything with a spoon. Usually anything that needs cutting can be busted apart, but every hiker should have one decent spoon. After a bad experience of stepping on and breaking my only plastic trail spoon, I became enamored of my metal, unbreakable trail gift. No amount of electrical tape or duct tape could repair my plastic spoon. I didn't want to borrow Rainmaker's spare. Stubbornly, I refused to take the spare. The trail gods stepped up and provided a regular teaspoon smack in the middle of a creek laying on a rock, north of Lassen Park, California.

Salt
A pinch of salt makes oatmeal, grits, pasta, rice, stew and just about any food taste way better. Bring a small vial with salt. Don't mix in pepper, though, because you might be adding it to the oatmeal in the morning.

There is nothing quite as relaxing as the aroma of brewing coffee. If you ever have to meet me at the mall, let's do it outside the Gourmet Coffee Shop. I'll be happily sitting on a bench, while the aroma drifts out. We might buy a cup of outrageously priced fresh brewed coffee, with a No-Fear-Of-Fat-Nor-Finances Double Chocolate Oreo Cookie Bar. You coffee addicts know what I mean. Those Sensory Stimulants can make a bad day turn around.

However, there are fewer options out on the trail. You can carry single serving prepackaged coffee bags. They come in boxes, just like tea bags and are for dunking in hot water. You can carry instant coffee, which is what I do because all of the weight is edible. Then you have the small pour-through cones with mesh filters to hold ground coffee. These cones work pretty well, but are a little bulky for such a single purpose item. Tea aficionados could use leaf tea in the cone, I guess.

But when all else fails, or even if nothing fails, you can make Cowboy Coffee. All you need is your pot, some boiling water, and regular ground coffee. If you happen upon a shelter, a hiker box, or grocery store, and all you find is regular coffee, you are still in business. Here is our tested and proven method. If you wish, you can strain it though a tiny device. I used one this summer in the Snowy Range The mug was used in basecamp. It was perfect.

Cowboy Coffee

Fill your pot 3/4 full with cold water. For every cup of water, measure one heaping tablespoon of regular coffee into the water. Bring to a boil, and continue to boil for 5 minutes. The longer you boil, the better the flavor. Remove from the heat. Let set a moment until the grounds settle. Pour slowly into your cup to avoid upsetting the grounds at the bottom. It is possible to filter it through a clean bandana. Keep in mind it will permanently color anything you use as a filter.

Gourmet Hot Cocoa

2 pounds cocoa powder
1 pound powdered sugar
1 12 ounce jar coffee creamer, your choice of flavor
6 cups instant powdered milk

Empty all ingredients into a large bowl or bucket. Mix well. Use 1/3 cup mix per cup of hot water. You can try various coffee creamers to vary the flavor.
This is an item to make ahead and portion into sandwich Ziploc baggies.

Coconut Cream Cocoa
---this I happened upon in Beldon, when I picked up some coconut cream powder
One package of coconut cream dessert powder
8 ounces hot cocoa instant powder

Empty powders into a quart size zip lock bag. Shake well to mix. Use 2 heaping tablespoons per 6 ounces of hot water.

Fruit Drink Powders

There are a lot of instant, fruit flavored, drink powders. Most contain a lot of sugar. Although the calories are fine, the weight of carrying the sugar should be considered. Take care the powder doesn't get wet or it will clump together. If that happens, you can break the clumps into manageable chunks and toss them in your water container where they can dissolve. If you are using iodine or chlorine, wait for the purification process before adding the powders. Some fruit drinks contain a vitamin C additive which will neutralize the iodine.

An alternative to carrying the heavy sugar is to use artificially sweetened varieties. This is a pure pleasure item because it doesn't provide calories, protein, or vitamins.

Jell-O powder, with sugar or artificial sweetener, makes a wonderful hot drink. Be sure to dissolve in hot water, stirring well to mix. If you like, you may mix it in a wide mouth jar. Leave it overnight and by morning, in the cool of the mountains, your Jell-O will set up. Once it's solid you can enjoy it with a spoon.

Covering Iodine

Iodine is a very lightweight method of purifying water. Use one tablet of aqua pure in a quart bottle. Shake to dissolve. Wait at least 1/2 hour before drinking. If the water is cold, it is better to wait several hours.

When you are ready to drink, you can place 1/2 vitamin C tablet in your bottle, and shake well. It will cover the iodine taste. The water will clarify and lose its yellowish color. However, don't add the vitamin C until you feel your water is purified. If the water source is questionable, err on the side of caution and give the iodine a little more time to work. The addition of the vitamin C will react chemically and stop any further purification. Some people find that their stomachs become upset with the addition of too much vitamin C because of the acid. It only takes a small amount, the smallest mg tablet you can find (100) cut in half.

Covering Chlorine

Two or three *drops* of regular household chlorine per liter of water is all that is needed to purify most water. When in doubt, allow the chlorine to work a little longer than the minimum of half an hour. The colder the water, the longer it takes for full purification benefits. If water is higher than 120 degrees, chlorine dissipates and becomes ineffectual in hot water. Direct sunlight also affects chlorine so until the half hour is up, leave water bottles in a shaded area.

If the water you are using has a lot of organic material in it, strain it first through a cotton bandana before adding drops of chlorine. On the Colorado Trail and in the cattle country in northern California of the Pacific Crest Trail, you'll find many water sources defiled by bovine feces. With few other alternatives, you may need to get water in one bottle, strain it into

16

another bottle, then add your choice of purifier. Those using a water filtering mechanical device will have to deal with it as well.

Some hikers put powdered fruit drinks into their chlorinated water after at least half an hour has passed for treatment. Powdered drink mixes can be hard to find in small trail towns. You may consider shipping yourself a variety of flavors in a bounce box, or having a friend mail you some periodically.

APPETIZERS

Tortilla and Cranberry Rollups
One wheat tortilla
cranberry or other fruit leather, about 1/4 cup

Heat tortilla in pot, in a zip lock bag in the sunshine, or over a campfire. While still warm, spread cranberry leather along one side of the tortilla and roll it up. Cover with cloth and allow the rollup to set a minute. Tastes really great.

Trail Mixes

Trail Mixes are any conglomeration of goodies that are placed in a Ziploc bag and can be eaten by handfuls while hiking, resting, cooking, or reading. The combinations vary as imagination allows. Below are some favorite ones of mine. As you can see, I do like to experiment with my food combinations.
Although many hikers will let friends reach in and grab a sample, this common practice can lead to serious illness. Studies have shown that poor hygiene, not bad water, causes most of the symptoms of intestinal sickness, such as diarrhea on the trail. I soon learned that when I want to share samples of my Trail Mix, I pour from the bag directly into the open hand. When sampling another hiker's stash, I ask for the same procedure by holding out my hand.

If this seems rude, remember you don't know how anyone conducts their personal hygiene. Getting sick on the trail can be serious stuff. With this debilitating possibility in mind, I now think twice about adopting an open bag of trail mixture from a hiker box.

Chocolate Trail Mix
One bag of chocolate chips
4 cups toasted oat cereal
2 cups raisins
4 cups peanuts

Pour the chips, cold cereal, raisins and peanuts into a gallon size Ziploc bag.. If it gets warm, the chips will melt. However, once it cools again, it will be in chunks. It is easier to eat when the chocolate is firm.

Soy Nut Trail Mix
3 cups roasted soy nuts
1 cup hulled sunflower seeds
1-cup almonds
1-cup honey roasted peanuts

Place all ingredients into a zip lock bag. This is very high in protein and fiber.

Maple Chex Trail Mix
---this one is a little more complicated because you actually have to use an oven. Make it ahead of your backpacking trip or day hike.

4 Tablespoons margarine
1/3-cup brown sugar
2 teaspoons maple extract
8 cups Chex cereal (any kind)
1-cup honey mixed nuts
1-cup pretzels (mini or stick)
2 cups M&Ms

Melt margarine in a saucepan. Stir in brown sugar and maple extract. In a large bowl, mix cereal, nuts and pretzels. Then add margarine mixture, stirring to coat everything. Place mixture on lightly sprayed cookie sheet. Bake at 225 degrees for 45 minutes, stirring every 15 minutes.

Remove from oven. Allow to cool. Add the M&Ms. Store in tightly sealed containers.

Dried Fruit Medley

I found this concoction in hiker box at Burney State Park and named it Monster Mash, contents, unknown.

This fruit mixture tasted surprisingly good.
The relative moisture of the dried prunes worked well with the apples.
The recipe represents my effort to reproduce that fantastic mix.

Coarse chop into a Ziploc bag, your choice of dried fruits: apples, bananas, prunes, raisins, dates, pineapple bits, orange peel, orange slices, and apricots. Shake to mix.
¼ cup of this medley can be added to hot cereals in the morning for breakfast, or rolled in a flour tortilla. It can also be eaten by handfuls but it can become sticky, especially on a warm day. You might decide to eat it with your spoon.

Ramen Trail Mix

Unbelievably good, ramen noodles without the seasoning packages are very interesting, and not too salty. Break ramen noodle squares into fourths, and place in a Ziploc bag. Add mixed nuts to the bag to increase protein and for variety.

Because ramen is a dehydrated food, be sure to drink a lot of water to aid in digestion.

Ramen noodle stats per 3 ounce dry noodles:
Protein...8 grams
Fat.... 16 grams
calories... 380

Honey Glazed Trail Mix

4 cups corn Chex
1 1/2 cup miniature pretzels
1 sup mixed nuts
1/3-cup margarine
1/3-cup honey

In a large saucepan, melt margarine and honey together. You may also do this in a bowl in the microwave.
Gradually stir in Chex, pretzels and nuts to mix well. Spread in jellyroll pan that has been coated with a non-sticking pan spray.

Bake at 350 degrees for 12-15 minutes, or until lightly glazed. Stir every few minutes so it will cook evenly.
Remove from oven and allow to cool completely. Store in Ziploc bags.

Here's a combination I happened upon in Beldon.

Beldon is a small "town" you pass through in northern California while hiking the Pacific Crest Trail. It has a small grocery store, terrific restaurant and rustic cabins available for rent. We paid $54 for the night in 2000, which seemed high at the time, but in retrospect, really wasn't. Our cabin had a fully functioning kitchen and coffee pot. The Post Office was a mile walk down the road. There are no facilities by the post office.
If you are planning to hike through that area, check current stats. Things often change in little towns.

After stashing our packs in the cabin, we headed to the little store. While slowly walking up and down the 3 grocery aisles, searching for food to resupply for Old Station, 88 miles away, the sole employee on duty took pity on me. I had traversed the entire store 4 times, shaking my head, figuring out a plan of action. There was just not enough food for four days. I saw one bag of white rice (cooking time 20 minutes), two Ramen in a Cup. No instant coffee. Some rye bread in a deep freezer. Dry cereal packaged in single kid sized servings. I paused and picked up half her entire stock of pop tarts (all four) and a one-pound tray of cookies.

Finally, after watching this for a few minutes, the lady looked at me and said quietly, "There are some hiker boxes on the back porch".
I smiled. I was in shorts and a tank top. How did she know I was a Hiker? This was my first introduction to serious resupply via hiker boxes.

I thanked her and went out the back screen door to take a look. There on the porch sat three medium sized cardboard boxes brimming with stuff others must have shipped to themselves via post office. They apparently knew the score here, but not wanting to carry any excess weight, they left behind their surpluses.

I set my Human Pride and Bag Lady Stereotypes aside, rolled up my imaginary hiker sleeves and dove in. One treasure I bagged is described as Candy Trail Mix.

Candy Trail Mix
m&ms
cinnamon bear juggie fruits
lemon drops
spice drops
candy corn
jelly beans (particularly black ones, if you can find them)

Dump all these candies together into a gallon Ziploc bag. Do not use any chocolate covered kinds, or they will melt over everything. That's another trail mix entirely. While hiking, you can enjoy the mixture as a game, like guessing what you have just popped into your mouth. Do not bite into it, until you are sure it doesn't contain a lemon drop. Very energizing and interesting.

From My Pacific Crest Trail Journal

"A Word about the Bag- I have noticed this phenomenon among many long distance hikers.
 A gallon size Ziploc bag is filled with a decent recipe of Gorp. Perhaps peanut M&Ms, walnuts, raisins, and yogurt covered dates.
 It's an enormous amount of food, so cannot be finished before the next resupply.

Perhaps a package of pretzels or a hiker box find of sesame sticks and sunflower seeds is then thrown into The Bag at the next town stop. Better to carry one large snack bag than several tads of food.
Next we find leftover Chex breakfast cereal joining The Bag. Or some "Does anyone want these apricots" joins The Bag.

One noted bag made it all the way from Idyllwild to Kennedy Meadows, 423 trail miles, where it was put into a hiker box. Within 2 hours another hiker claimed it. Thankfully, that hiker finished it by Vermillion Valley.

No way on God's green earth could recipes ever be written for a 300 mile bag. It may be the most awesome of trail mixes: including shredded coconut, freeze dried strawberries, corn and peas. Included but not limited to Captain Crunch, Kandy Korn, peanuts, bacon crackers, and corn nuts. It's not a matter of imagination. It's a matter of no Ziplocs. Well, that and convenience. At snack time, just haul out The Bag and chow. If holes develop, as in even the best of bags, a duct tape patch is used. The crumbs are not thrown away, but eaten, regardless of salt or sugar concentration."

Heirloom Hardtack
This recipe was discovered in an article about the Civil War. It piqued my curiosity. If soldiers could live on this stuff while carrying heavy packs, wouldn't it be perfect for the backpacker on a budget?

Basic Hardtack
1 ½ cups milk
2 cups white flour
2 cups whole-wheat flour
2 tablespoons brown sugar
1 ½ teaspoons salt

Mix the ingredients into a firm dough, then roll it out to a thickness of about 1/2 inch. Cut into squares. Place squares on greased cookie sheets and prick each one with a fork.

Or, you can grease a jellyroll pan, and simply press dough into it. Cut into squares while in the pan. Prick the dough with a fork. Bake at 375 degrees for 20-30 minutes, until golden brown.

If hardtack is cooked until nearly brittle, it will last a long time. Supposedly, Union soldiers carried and ate hardtack from the War of 1812 when they marched south in 1861.

We tried the basic recipe and found them to be quite tasty. Just be careful not to break a tooth biting off a chunk. They didn't name these "hard" for nothing.

In an effort to come up with some flavors for this heirloom recipe, I started with a few standard ingredients. Below are some of the best results.

Cinnamon Banana Hardtack
2 very ripe bananas
2 cups white flour
2 tablespoons brown sugar
1 teaspoons salt
1 teaspoon cinnamon
1 tablespoon oil

Mix the ingredients into a stiff dough and knead gently for 3 minutes.

Spray a 9x13-baking pan with non-stick pan spray, and press dough into it.
Cut into squares while in the pan.
Prick the dough with a fork.
Bake at 375 degrees for 20-30 minutes, until golden brown. Turn off oven, let set for an additional 10 minutes to draw out additional moisture.
Remove from oven and allow to cool. When cool, store in a zip lock bag.

Cheesy Hardtack
2 cups cheese sauce
4 cups white flour
1 teaspoons salt
1-teaspoon garlic powder

Mix the ingredients into dough and knead gently for 3 minutes.
Spray a sheet pan with non-stick pan spray, and press dough into it.
Cut into squares while in the pan. Prick the dough with a fork.
Bake at 375 degrees for 20-30 minutes, until golden brown. Turn off oven, let set for an additional 10 minutes.
When cool, store in a zip lock bag.

BREAKFAST

The Annual Kick Off Party held at Lake Moreno. Northbound thru hikers congregate at the campground, just 20 miles north of the Mexican border, right off the Pacific Crest Trail. This event is held the last weekend in April. The year I did the trail, food was provided by trail angles and friends. It was really fun meeting everyone there, seeing all the homemade gear and feeling the moral support for the continuation of an epic journey.

Breakfast is considered to be the most important meal of the day. If you're a night hiker, or on the night shift, the first meal you eat after sleeping is really "breaking your fast." This first meal after spending 8 or more hours in your tent recovering from a long hard day of backpacking should help replenish calories and energy stores.

I have witnessed a thru-hiker on the Pacific Crest Trail simply roll over from under his ground-tarp, grab some fixing's from around his head, pour them into his dish, add water and commence eating. This is called Breakfast-in-A-Tarp. Some of the Glorified Cold Cereals would lend themselves to this method.

Another practice used to achieve big mile days, is to pack up camp and eat a Power Breakfast on the move. The Breakfast Bar in this section works well, too. Try an Instant Shake or a fruit drink, found in the Beverages section of this book, to add extra calories.

As an ultralighter, I wake up quickly on cold mornings and get moving. I know that once I start hiking, I'll warm up. As a minimalist with not much to pack, I can accomplish this quickly, while leaving my breakfast bar nearby so I can eat it while getting in those first miles.

Everybody loves Fast food

Really, not everyone does love fast food or a fast departure from camp.

My hiking partner hates this packing up and eating on the run. He will not leave without having his coffee first.

When hiking through Glacier National Park and the Bob Marshall where Grizzly Bears are a concern, I would lay warm in my sleeping bag while Rainmaker went through his morning routine away from camp. This seemed like a lot of work to me, so I'd sleep in, then jump up when he returned from breakfast. When I knew we were about to leave, I'd pull out my pop tart from the bear canister and eat on the go.

For those of you who have the time, inclination and intense need for a Caffeine hit, hot breakfasts abound. When I do a sit down for breakfast, I heat water for coffee immediately and make my 8 ounces of java as quickly as possible. Then, while sipping it, I make sense of the general disorder of my gear. I'll heat more water, then and use it for instant hot cereals.If you want pancakes for breakfast, there are recipes for them in the **Breads** section of this cookbook.

25

Malted Breakfast Shake

Measure equal amounts of each ingredient into a large Ziploc bag:
powdered milk
instant malted milk powder
hot cocoa powder (sweetened)

For every 2 cups of water, measure about 2/3 cup of powder. Add powder to the water in your bottle. Shake vigorously. This

Favorite Camp Latte
Two teaspoons instant coffee
One teaspoon cocoa powder
One-third (1/3) cup powdered milk
Two artificial sweetener packages
Dash of salt

Stir all ingredients in a cup. Add very hot water. Stir to mix. I actually enjoy this beverage at home too. It has the anti-oxidants of cocoa and coffee, and 9 grams of protein.

Breakfast Bars
There are a lot of ingredients for this recipe, but they are well worth the effort. Make a double batch, cut, wrap and freeze them for easy, on the go, high protein bars.

1 cup shortening
1 cup white sugar
1 cup brown sugar
1/3 cup peanut butter
2 eggs
1 teaspoon baking soda
1/2 teaspoon baking powder
1/2 teaspoon salt
1 teaspoon vanilla
2 cups flour
1 cup chocolate chips
1 cup quick cooking oatmeal
1 cup Rice Crispies cereal
1 cup sweetened coconut

In a large bowl, mix shortening, white and brown sugars, peanut butter and eggs.

Add baking soda, baking powder, salt, and vanilla. Mix well. Stir in flour and chocolate chips. Then add oatmeal, Rice Crispies, and coconut. Mix well.

Grease a jellyroll pan and press dough evenly into it. Bake at 375 degrees for about 10-12 minutes.

Do not over bake. They will set up, or get firm, while cooling. Bakers call this "residual heat" and "carry over cooking." Who knew?

Power-start Bars
1 cup brown sugar
1/2 cup vegetable oil
2 cups instant oats
1 1/2 cups whole wheat flour
1 cup raisins or dates
1 cup chopped nuts
1 cup flaked coconut
1 1/2 teaspoons cinnamon
1/2 teaspoon ground cloves
1 teaspoon baking powder
1/4 teaspoon salt

Blend sugar, oil and spices together. Stir in the flour and oats. Add the coconut and raisins and dates, if desired. Mix well.

Lightly grease or coat with anti-stick pan spray a 15 x 10 inch x 1 inch deep bar pan. Press mixture into it. Bake at 350 degrees until lightly browned, about 17-22 minutes.

Remove from oven. Allow to cool for 10 minutes. Cut into bars before they are totally cold.

Glorified Rice Chex
Into a gallon size zip lock bag, empty:
one 13 ounce bag of rice chex cereal
one 3 ounce box of pistachio pudding mix (powder)
1 cup dry (powdered) milk

Before using, shake well, and then pour the amount desired into your dish. Pour water to cover. Stir well.

Other pudding mixes may be used. This happened to be the flavor I found in Ashland, Oregon from a previous hiker box raid. It does sound weird, but it's delicious.

Granola
Measure into a large micro-wavable bowl:
5 tablespoons margarine or canola oil
1/2 cup packed brown sugar.

Set time to 12 minutes, full power.
Microwave margarine and brown sugar for about 45 seconds.
Remove bowl from microwave and stir in:
4 cups oatmeal
1 cup wheat germ
1 ½ cups sweetened coconut
1 cup hulled sunflower seeds

Continue microwaving and cooking granola for the remaining time. Every few minutes remove the bowl from the microwave and carefully stir the contents. Pay special attention to the bottom so it doesn't burn and to promote even browning. When 10 minutes of microwaving time have elapsed, check and stir more frequently. Granola will crisp and darken as it cools.

After 12 minutes are done, more or less depending on your microwave, remove bowl from microwave and allow granola to cool. Stir to permit steam to escape.

You can add dried fruit at this time. A 15-ounce box of raisons or dried cranberries is great. When totally cool, store in airtight container.

Using the oven instead:
This same recipe can be made in a regular oven. Place all ingredients, except the dried fruit, in a large bowl. Use melted margarine or oil to facilitate mixing.

Pour your mixture onto large baking sheet and bake in 325 degree oven, stirring occasional, until browned. Watch this carefully or it will burn. Cooking time depends on thickness of mixture on baking sheet. Stir to obtain even browning. I find the microwave method quicker and more dependable.

Granola can be cooked with water while on the trail if you want something hot. This high calorie cereal makes a substantial supper if you're getting low or sick of pasta dishes. Use ½ cup granola for each cup of water. Add more for thicker cereal.

Corn Meal Magic
Each 1/4-cup of cornmeal contains 100 calories, 2 grams of protein, and 1 gram of fat. I prefer to use cornmeal instead of corn pasta because it is easier to find, easier to cook, and is more dense, meaning there is more food value for the volume.

Bring 1 cup water to a boil.
Gradually stir in ½ cup self-rising corn meal. Turn off your heat and continue to stir until it is thickened. If you cannot find self-rising use regular, but add a dash of salt to bring out the flavor.

You can garnish the cornmeal mush with cheese, honey, or jelly. Add bacon bits for an interesting breakfast or anytime trail meal.

Grits
A one-ounce package of instant grits contains 100 calories, 2 grams of protein, and one gram of fat. If you buy regular grits, they'll take longer to cook, but still pack well, providing a lot of food for the volume.

There are many flavors of instant grits. If you buy the plain variety, prepare them by heating 1 ¼ cups of water in your pot. Slowly empty 2 packages of instant grits into your water, stirring well.
Add 2 tablespoons milk powder, cheese or butter and dash of salt and pepper if desired.
Grits make an easy, fast supper too.

Oatmeal
One third cup of quick cooking oats contains 150 calories, 5 grams of protein, and 3 grams of fat.

For these recipes, use the quick cooking oats which take only one minute to prepare.
Although most stores have instant prepackaged oatmeal cereal, with various flavors, sometimes the cost is outrageous. At the Burney Falls State Park store in the summer of 2000, one single once serving cost 85 cents. If you are resupplying for a week, and eat two each breakfast, that alone would be $11.90. Plus tax. Instead, you can just buy a box of quick oats and add some flavors.

When cooking oatmeal, heat your water first, then pour in the oatmeal and stir once or twice. If you stir it too much, it will become pasty. Or you can heat water to boiling and pour over oatmeal which has been measured into a plastic container. Cover and let it set for a few minutes. Add a dash of salt and sweetener and stir. This method keeps your pot available for heating water for coffee while you enjoy your oatmeal.

Oatmeal and Raisins
Makes one hiker serving

2/3 cups quick cooking oatmeal
1/4 teaspoon cinnamon
1/3 cup raisins
dash of salt
white or brown sugar to taste, about 1-2 teaspoons

Measure all of the ingredients into a zip lock bag. For each hiker serving, heat 1 1/3 cups water to almost boiling. Pour in cereal mixture, stirring only once or twice. Cover and let stand for 3 minutes. It will thicken as it cools.

Oatmeal, Peaches and Cream
2/3 cups quick cooking oatmeal
2 tablespoons dry (powdered) milk
1/4 teaspoon cinnamon
dash of nutmeg
1/3 cup dried peaches, broken into bits
dash of salt
1 teaspoon butter buds
white or brown sugar to taste, about 1-2 teaspoons

Place all of the ingredients into a Ziploc bag. This makes one hungry- hiker serving. Heat 1 1/3 cups water to near boil. Pour in contents of bag, stirring just a time or two. Cover and allow to stand for 3 minutes. It will thicken and the peaches will rehydrate in this time, as it cools.

Oatmeal with an Attitude

Per each Hiker serving:
1/2 cup instant oats
1 teaspoon butter buds
1/4 teaspoon cinnamon
5 banana chips, broken up
2 dried apple rings, broken up likewise
a handful of raisins
1 teaspoon white or brown sugar
1 tablespoon powdered milk

Into a Ziploc bag place all ingredients. Shake well. If you have multiple servings in a large bag, be sure to shake well every time before measuring out your portion.

Bring 1 ¼ cups of water to a boil. Add dry oatmeal mixture to water. Stir only once. If you over stir oatmeal it turns pasty. Cover and let sit for 3 minutes.

Cream of Wheat

Each one-ounce serving has 100 calories, 2 grams of protein, and no fat. Cream of wheat looks a lot like grits, but it is smoother and made from wheat, not corn as is grits.

Bring 1 1/2 cups of water to a boil. Very slowly and gently, stir in 1/3 cup quick cooking cream of wheat. Stir until it thickens. Cover, let set two minutes. Serve with dash of salt, and sugar to taste.

Monster Mash

This recipe originated when I found a Ziploc bag of mysterious dried fruits at Burney State Park, California. One morning, I was hungrier than usual and took a handful of this mash to fortify the simple oats I was preparing.

It was amazing how good the fruit tasted in hot cereal. A tortilla spread with peanut butter and sprinkled liberally with monster mash, makes a great snack or breakfast, also.

Suggestions for the mash include, but are not limited to: Raisons, dates prunes, figs, dried pineapple, peaches, apricots, dried apples, dried orange peels, and mixed nuts, finely chopped.

31

Chop all dried fruits into small pieces. Add to the Ziploc bag any and all of the ones you can find. The prunes will cause the others to moisten somewhat, but this is no problem. Add the mixed nuts, and store in a cool dry place, in the refrigerator or freezer.

Putting Pop tarts in their Place

Brand name Poptarts are great. Well, I think so anyways but I know they have a bad reputation for tasting like cardboard. I admit, once I bought some generic ones at a grocery store in Mohave. It wasn't that there were no brand name poptarts. I was thinking, "How bad can a poptart be, a tarts a tart."

Not so. Be sure to buy the frosted ones. It really helps the flavor, in my opinion, of the pastry part. Brand names tend to have more filling too, a real plus when that's what's on your breakfast menu day after day.

The upside of this prepackaged pastry is that they are generally available in convenience stores, there are flavors to choose from, and they have plenty of calories. To enhance their flavor, you may choose to spread peanut butter, jelly, or canned frosting on them. If possible, warm them on top of the lid of your pot while making your morning coffee.

One trick is to break poptarts into your pot, add a few raisins, 2 tablespoons dry milk. Add just enough water and eat them just like cold breakfast cereal.

Often we would find many single packages of poptarts in hiker boxes all along the way. After the poptarts are out of the box, there are no labels on the silver wrapping so we dubbed them "Mystery Tarts".

In retrospect, haven't met a Tart that I didn't like while on the trail. However, I will always buy the ones with frosting and the spring for the brand name over the generic when possible.

Breakfast Burrito
Instant eggs
Salsa
Tortillas

I hiked with a guy up in the Moroon Bells, near Aspen, Colorado. He created this breakfast burrito within minutes and gave me a taste. It's a decent alternative to cereal or poptarts. Look for eggs with seasoning if you can.

Here I am, heading north on a cold dreary day, March 15th, from Springer Mountain, Georgia, the southern terminus of the Appalachian Trail.
A person uses more calories when it's cold, and it improves morale knowing there's plenty of food in the bag. Photo taken by David Mauldin.

Soups are an easy appetizer and staves off hunger when you sit down to cook. Eating soup also helps you rehydrate. Warm water is absorbed quicker than cold.

I've learned that a few dabs of this and that and the tiniest bit of instant foods can create a meal if they're added to near boiling water with a bouillon cube.

If you're heading to town in the morning, utilize these scraps in a recipe I call **Desperation Soup**. The story behind it can be found with the recipe that follows these tried and true trail recipes.

Cream of Potato Soup
1/3 cup instant mashed potatoes
1 tablespoon instant dry milk powder
1 teaspoon chicken bouillon
1/8 teaspoon garlic powder
1/8 teaspoon sage
1/4 teaspoon minced onions
1 Tablespoon of parmesan cheese, if you have it

Place all the ingredients in a sandwich size Ziploc bag except the bouillon cube. Make multiple servings by doubling or quadrupling the recipe, mixing them all in a quart size bag.

When you want to make the soup, bring one cup water to a near boil. Add 1/2 cup of the mixture and stir a few minutes until it thickens.

If you have multiplied the recipe, be sure to shake well before measuring out a 1/2-cup portion for one serving.
This instant soup mix can be enhanced with croutons and shredded cheese for a heartier meal.

Other additions include dehydrated vegetables and bite sized or crumbled dried meats or bacon bits.

Cream of Asparagus Soup
1/2 cup instant mashed potatoes
1/2-cup dry (powdered) milk
1 cup dehydrated asparagus pieces (see chapter on dehydrating vegetables)
1/2-teaspoon garlic
1/4-teaspoon salt
1/4-teaspoon pepper
1 envelope butter buds or a squeeze of oil

Measure all ingredients into a sandwich size ziploc bag. Shake well to mix. Bring 2 cups of water to a near boil. Stir in half the contents of this mix. Lower, or turn off heat. Cover tightly and allow carry over cooking for 5 minutes.
This vegetarian soup is fairly hearty and perfect with Parmesan cheese sprinkled on top.

Split Pea Soup
1/4 cup split peas, finely ground in a blender
1/4 teaspoon salt
1 teaspoon chicken bouillon
1/8 teaspoon garlic powder
dash of black pepper
1/4 cup dry milk powder

Mix the peas, salt, bouillon powder and spices.
Pour finely ground split pea soup mix into a watertight container. Add 1 ¼ cups of water. Allow to soak for 4 hours. You can use your Nalgene bottle or similar wide mouth bottle for this. Combine the ingredients on your lunch break and it will be ready in time for supper.

After the mixture has soaked, pour it into your pot. Bring to a boil and simmer until soup is thickened and peas are tender. The finer ground the peas are, the quicker this will happen, about 5-8 minutes. Add dry milk powder just before eating, stir to blend

There are 17 grams of protein but no fat in this recipe. Garnish with bacon bits and croutons for a very satisfying meal.

Adding oil enhances flavor of both soups and stews. Fats boost the calorie count and take longer to digest, providing more satisfaction. Bring canola oil or olive oil in liquid safe containers, which are well sealed.

As a precaution, place the plastic bottle in a solid plastic bag as well, and store away from clothing.

Desperation Soup

This soup is made from all the odds and ends of the food bag. I always keep at least one "seasoning" package from my ramen noodles just in case.

Into the boiling water, you can add instant mashed potatoes, instant rice, pasta crumbs, dehydrated beans and edible foliage like wild onions and nettles.
I never throw out the crumbs of anything until I hit town and resupply. Garnish the soup with crackers, chips, pretzels or whatever you have on hand.

This recipe has seen me through more than once. The most vivid memory surfaces from the Colorado Trail where Rainmaker and I decided not to hitchhike to Silverton. We just seemed to have a hard time snagging a ride. Maybe we looked too wild.

As we approached Molas Pass, both of us silently considered the contents of our food bags. We always cooked separately, no matter how long or short the trail. I remembered some instant potatoes, a few ramen seasoning packages. A few crumbs, maybe, of pretzels.

Turns out, those few morsels would have to be a supper. The camp store didn't have any main courses, just snacks. The proprietor gave us some dehydrated beans and tortillas that a hiker had shipped to himself, but donated to hikers. She had put those goods in her home. She took pity on us and offered the two items. I quickly accepted. Rainmaker and I split that.

We had just five nights left on the trail. Two of those nights I made Desperation Soup and used pretzels to fill me up. It was a good experience and taught me how lucky I was to be an American and not have to do this every day of my life.

A typical photo shot of us, Rainmaker in a full beard, me in black.

Below, a photo of a camp pitched right on the trail, just before dusk.

Trailside Dumplings
1/4-cup self-rising flour
1-teaspoon oil
warm water to moisten

Mix flour, oil and water. Into boiling soup or broth, drop dumpling mixture by scant teaspoons. Continue boiling for 3 minutes. Simmer another 5 minutes. Turn off heat, cover well and allow to set 5 more minutes.

The trick is to drop small bits of dough into boiling stock so that it cooks quickly. If your water is not boiling, they will dissolve before cooking through.

Pasta Done Right
The trick to good pasta, whether you're on the trail, in town or at home, is plenty of boiling water. But, even if you don't have a very large pot you can still make decent pasta. I use this method to cook my ramen too, always heating the water first to a low boil before adding the noodles.

Angle hair, spaghetti, macaroni, flat egg noodles, shells, and spirals all make great alternatives to the tried and true, albeit bland Ramen we all know and love. I do steer clear of corn pasta or whole wheat pasta on the trail. Both take longer to cook, need more water per ounce of pasta and require a decent, consistent boil.

Begin by filling your pot with water and bringing it to a boil. You can add the salt at this time, if you like.

Break spaghetti into short lengths or add the other pasta to boiling water. Stir to break up the mass of pasta and prevent it from becoming stuck together. Allow pasta to cook until nearly tender, maintaining a low boil and adding water if necessary. This low boil keeps the pasta from simmering into a pasty mess.

By now your fuel is probably running out.
Remove from heat, leave the cover on and insulate for a few minutes to take advantage of carry over cooking, or residual heat.

Lift lid, drain excess water. Add a squirt of oil if you have it, seasoning, salt, and cheese if available.

Heat & Serve Quick Dinner
--Submitted by Rainmaker

This is an old stand-by dinner that I never seem to get tired of. All the ingredients were cooked (before you bought them), so all that is necessary is rehydrating your dinner to make it palatable, and heating it to make it taste good. The Knorr Black Bean Soup is the kind that comes in Styrofoam cups at supermarkets.

The following portions will satisfy one hungry long-distance hiker, or maybe 2 normal people:
1 package Ramen noodles
1 cup instant rice
Several ounces Knorr Black Bean Soup Mix
Spices / seasoning of choice
1 ounce (or more) Parmesan cheese
1 1/2 - 2 cups water

Combine all ingredients in your pot (except the Parmesan cheese), and let it soak for 15 minutes. This will allow all contents to rehydrate. I don't like Ramen seasoning packets (any of them), so I generally discard them. My favorite spices for this meal are curry powder, garlic salt, lemon/ pepper and/or a packet of Lipton Instant Cup-O-Soup.

If you are in a hurry for dinner, mix all the ingredients and let them rehydrate while you are putting up your tent and unpacking the rest of your stuff.

After rehydrating, bring contents to a boil, then reduce heat and simmer for 2 or 3 minutes. Remove from heat and allow it to sit for 5 minutes, then garnish with Parmesan cheese and enjoy. What could be easier?

Mexican Ramen
Hot and Spicy Ramen flavor noodles
1/2 cup dehydrated tomatoes
1 tablespoon dried, minced onions (sold as a spice)
sharp cheddar cheese, broken or sliced into small chunks

Place 2 cups water in your pot. Add tomatoes and onions. Bring to a simmer, add noodles and spice package. Stir well, cover and allow to set for 4 minutes. Add chunks of sharp cheddar cheese.

Ramen Italiano

Beef flavored Ramen Noodles
1/4 cup dehydrated tomato sauce
1/4 cup dehydrated ground beef if desired
dash each of minced onions and garlic powder
parmesan cheese

Place 2 cups water in your pot.
Add tomato sauce and the spices. Bring to a simmer. Add beef flavoring package and noodles. Add the dehydrated beef. Stir well to blend. Cover and allow to set for 4 minutes.
Just before eating, sprinkle generously with Parmesan cheese.

Ramen Alfredo
--makes two servings
One envelope Alfredo sauce mix
one envelope butter buds
1/2 cup dry (powdered) milk
3 packages ramen noodles, broken up

Place all ingredients in a quart size ziploc bag. Shake to mix.

To cook, put two cups of water in your pot. Heat to nearly boiling, then stir in half of this mixture. Continue to cook until noodles are done and sauce has thickened.

You can use angel hair pasta instead of Ramen for the recipes above. I've even used spaghetti for a while on the AT. It takes longer to cook, though, and if you're really tired, you might actually fall asleep while it cooks.
One day after hiking 20 miles, I climbed into the shelter, leaned against the wall and started cooking. The Massachusetts Four were there, and we had been enjoying some good conversation along the way.
My water came to a boil so I broke my pasta into bite size pieces and dropped it in, stirred it a couple times and put the lid on.
I closed my eyes. Next thing I knew, I woke with a start, turned sideways, totally forgetting my supper. Instantly I knocked it over, into the dirt below the shelter flooring.

It was so perfectly cooked, al dente and perfectly tender. I frowned, jumped up and started scraping it out of the dirt and into my pot. One of my friends saw it and said, "I have an extra ramen."

"That's ok," I replied, embarrassed. "I'm just going to put this in the outhouse pit."

He brought over the package, said, "No, take it, I'm not going to need it. In fact, I'm not going to carry it anymore, either."

I just didn't want to do it, taking someone's food, but he held the ramen.

"Ok," I said, relenting. "Thanks." I learned, if you're really tired, cook while standing up and moving around.

Instant Rice

---Stats per 1/2 cup uncooked rice: 180 calories; no fat; 4 grams of protein. Instant rice can be eaten raw in a pinch.

Use equal amounts of water and Instant Rice. Be sure what you have is instant and not quick cooking or plain white rice. Regular white rice requires 20 minutes cooking time. Regular brown rice needs 50.

Heat water in pot. Add an equal amount of Instant Rice. Stir in flavorings, and a dash of salt. Cover and remove from heat. Let stand for a few minutes for better texture.

If you have bouillon cubes, dehydrated chili, tomatoes or Alfredo sauce mix, rice can be very good. Sprinkle Parmesan cheese on your cooked rice and it will be even better.

You can eat rice for breakfast, too. Cook it completely, then add raisins, cinnamon and sugar. Pour rehydrated milk over this as you would a breakfast cereal.

A Corn Meal Casserole Story

At Burney Falls State Park we were disheartened by the prices. The grill seemed expensive. So did the store. Our accommodations cost $3 a night each, which was a campsite with no water and very little shade.

We had hiked there from Old Station, thru the Hat Creek Rim. A half-gallon of ice cream would have gone down real easy right now, but there was none. A 12-ounce soda was 85 cents. No two liters. Bummer. It was 83 miles to Dunsmuir.

Not wanting to hitch hike down to Burney Falls, Rainmaker and I settled into the dilemma of getting a bite to eat and resupplying for five days. I asked the clerk if they had Hiker Boxes. Yes, she said, they did, but could we please take it out behind, away from the grill area?

I took the box, thanked the lady and headed outside. The Out Behind had just been claimed by a lady with kids, so I brought the box to Rainmaker who was sitting at one of the picnic tables smack dab in front of the grill. Quickly we sorted through every last thing. One thing Rain picked up was Corn Mush with Green Peas.

Over the years I've changed my outlook on prices in remote locations. In reality, I'm glad someone is selling food and drink at all. It costs money to run an operation like that, so I try not to complain anymore about the sticker price.

Early the next morning, we loaded up our gear and food supplies and headed out. Each night we would cook something unnamed and mysterious, pouring ingredients from sandwich bags into two cups of boiling water. I ended up with a lot of corn pasta. He ended up with a lot of rice, and one serving of Corn Mush with Green Peas.

One night, after a long 18-mile day to a scanty water source and discovering a campsite on an old logging road above the trail where the guide book emphatically warned there was none, Rainmaker drug out the Corn Mush...With Green Peas. The peas were little green dehydrated things. I think even perhaps straight from a split pea bag for 33 cents. I glanced at the bag and thought, someone's sweetheart must have concocted this, perhaps even a mom wanting her boy to eat his peas, come hell or high water.

Anyways, I cooked my pasta as best as corn pasta can be cooked. Rainmaker leaned against his tree, dumped his mixture into his pot with enough water to cover it all. Casually he lit an esbit tablet and set his pot over the flame. I glanced over occasionally as he stirred the contents.

After the esbit tablet finished burning 13 minutes later, he took a bite. I could hear the peas in his mouth, like gravel in a plastic cup.
"How is it?" I asked.

He gave me a sour look and lit another esbit tablet. I suggested he add more water. The food in his pot was thick and solid because the corn meal had cooked long ago and turned into a thickened mass, yet the peas were still stubborn as rocks.

I could smell the bottom of the pot beginning to burn in spite of constant stirring. The second fuel tablet burned completely. He stuck his spoon into the pot, raised it to his mouth, and took another bite. A look of disgust came over his face. He tried to eat another spoonful. More gravely noise.

Things were not good. I felt the tension all the way over to my pot of pasta, just finished. We were tired, hungry and in bear country. Rainmaker stood and did the only thing he could do. Picking up his pot by the pot lifter, he walked away. When he came back fifteen minutes later, he said he had walked 1/2 mile down the trail and buried it. Then he said he scrubbed the burned corn meal from the bottom of the pot.

Rainmaker sat down, frowned, looked around wearily. He got up and headed out, remembering he'd forgotten his pot lifter down by the water where he had scrubbed the pot.

"Would you like me to cook you something?" I meekly asked. "No!" he replied as he went to retrieve his essential pot lifter.

When he returned, I watched him make a cup of coffee, eat a candy bar. Darkness had settled in and we went to bed.

Moral of story is don't combine things that take a long time to cook to things that take very little time to cook. Peas like this need to be soaked overnight or ground to powder. The corn meal will cook almost instantly. So, now with that lesson learned, here is a recipe for some good corn meal eating, at suppertime.

Cheesy Cornmeal Delight
3/4-cup self-rising corn meal
1 1/2 cups water
cheese, Parmesan, or block cheese broken into small bits
2 ounces of beef sticks/ salami, chopped into chunks

Put the water and beef chunks into your pot. Bring water to a boil. Add the corn meal slowly, stirring constantly. Turn off heat. Add the cheese on top. It is ready to enjoy.

Cornmeal and Peas

1/4 cup split peas, ground into fine powder in a blender
1/2 cup corn meal
1 chicken bouillon cube
1 teaspoon butter buds
½ teaspoon salt
dash chili powder
dash garlic powder
dash black pepper

Combine all ingredients into a ziploc bag.
To cook, add corn and pea mixture to 2 cups water and heat until simmering. Continue to cook until thickened and peas are tender. Because they have been ground to a powder, they will cook much faster than in the original split pea state.

Chili Cornmeal with Cheese

½ cup dehydrated chili
¾ cup corn meal
¼ cup cheese leather, broken into bits, or use block cheese when meal is cooked

Combine chili and cornmeal in a ziploc bag. If you have the cheese leather, add that also.
To cook, add corn and chili mixture to 2 cups water and heat until simmering. Continue cooking until thickened. If you are adding cubed block cheese, put it in the pot and cover. Allow to set for 3 minutes. Stir to blend melted cheese.

Hikers Stew

Dehydrating vegetables and meats for backpacking stew mixes is a great way to utilize leftover cooked foods at home. Dehydrate boiled or scalloped potatoes and add them to the mix for a hearty stew.

Place well-drained cooked vegetables on several dehydrator trays. Arrange similar sized pieces of food closely together. They will shrink remarkably, so it's a good idea to have a large quantity to make it worth the effort. Any kind of vegetable makes a good candidate, including broccoli, cauliflower, sliced or cubed boiled potatoes, onions, and beans. Peas become almost invisible when dried, but they can still be used.

Meats for stew mixes may be done at the same time. I like to use another tray and put it at the bottom of the stack to avoid meat juices dripping on the vegetables.

Slice the meat into small 1/4-inch strips. Roast beef, hamburger, chicken, and turkey are some favorites. These basic meats are very versatile and can be cooked with pasta, rice or as soup.

Use cooked meats for the stew mixes. Dehydrating raw meats is fine for jerky, but it doesn't rehydrate well in stew.

Place vegetables and meat pieces on dehydrator trays. Choose the meat setting, or hottest setting, if your dehydrator has one. I have used a simple machine with no blower and it worked fine. The key is to rotate the trays after twelve hours because the bottom tray will dehydrate faster than the top one. Especially when doing meat, it is important to encourage even, quick dehydrating. This procedure prevents bacterial growth.

When all the items are completely dry, combine and divide into snack size Ziploc bags. You may want to break the meat into smaller chunks at this time.

Into each single serving baggie place:
Dehydrated stew combination, about ¾ cup
1 unwrapped bouillon cube
1/4 teaspoon Garlic powder
2 tablespoons flour or cornstarch
pinch of black pepper.

To cook, pour contents into 2 cups of cold water, stirring well to dissolve flour or cornstarch. Bring to boil, stirring while flour or cornstarch thickens and bubbles.

Ramen noodles, instant rice, or croutons may be added at this time.

Mashed Potatoes and Meat Flavored Gravy
The stats for this meal is a combination of both the instant potatoes and gravy mix. For 1/3-cup potato flakes: 80 calories; no fat; 2 grams of protein. Add that to gravy mix stats, per 2 tablespoons dry mix: 20 calories; 1 gram of fat; 3 grams of protein.

4 tablespoons gravy mix (half of package)
1 cup potato flakes
2 tablespoons dry powdered milk

45

Heat 2 cups of water to a boil. Place 1/3 cup in a small container with the gravy mix. Stir well to blend.

Add the potato flakes and instant milk to the rest of the water. Mix well. Serve gravy over potatoes. This hiker meal-side dish delivers 14 grams of protein and 300 calories.

Potatoes Al Gratin con Carne
1 ½ cups water
2 ounces Beef Sticks, chopped into bites
1 ½ cups instant mashed potatoes
1 teaspoons chives
¼ cup dry (powdered) milk
block cheddar cheese, about one ounce
parmesan cheese

Measure the potatoes, chives, and milk powder into a ziploc bag for one serving. Multiply the recipe and put in quart ziploc, if you like.

To cook, first chop the beef stick into your pot. Add water and bring to near boil. Stir in contents of ziploc bag. Mix well. Break cheese into small bits and add them to the hot potatoes. Cover pot and allow to set a minute to melt cheese. Sprinkle with Parmesan if desired.

Veggie Burgers
1/3 cup quick cooking oats
1/3 cup ground split peas
1/3 cup self-rising cornmeal
2/3 cup self-rising white flour
1/4 cup dry (powdered) milk
1 tablespoon bouillon powder
dash of garlic powder
oil for frying
catsup, if you have it, as a garnish

Measure the oats, finely ground split peas, (you can use a blender to grind the peas), cornmeal, flour and dry milk into a ziploc bag.

The entire contents of this bag can be shaken well and 1/2 cup of warm water added to it. Allow to set for 5 minutes so the baking powder in the self-rising meals is activated. You can use regular flour or cornmeal but the resulting burger will be somewhat denser.

To cook, heat the oil in your pot, and fry each veggie burger on both sides, until nicely browned.
Serve with catsup or salsa. Makes 5 nice sized burgers, each having approximately 6 grams of protein.

I took a picture of this dude named Falafel who told me a mouse gave birth in his pack while he slept at Low Gap Shelter, on the Appalachian Trail.
He admitted he didn't have the heart to evict the new family, so he waited until she moved out on her own, later that day.

Meat

On the trail or while camping, any kind of meat must be treated with great respect. Without proper storage, serious illness can develop. Without proper cooking, food borne illness can force you to seek medical attention.

Any product that is high in protein and moisture is considered a potentially dangerous food. With proper handling, this tremendous source of protein can be enjoyed.

My whimsical sketch of bears trying to catch a ride to Smokey Mountain National Park. I remembered times we'd stand by the road, thumbs out. Sometimes another hiker might appear, upstaging our efforts.

Many hikers look forward to their town stops for days, imagining the ice cream, burgers and steaks. Meanwhile, they go easy on the trail because of the difficulty in safe handling of meat, plus the odorous nature of fish, chicken and beef can attract bears.

You can carry prepackaged beef sticks. These are vacuum-sealed and are not beef jerky. Once open, the wrappers smell very beefy. I ended up burning my wrappers during lunch break after several evenings of roaming bear visitations.

Beef jerky is another option for the backpacker. Some meat lovers will take the time to dry ground beef, ground turkey or chicken for cooking purposes. They like making it themselves because they can control the spices and salts in each product, and feel confident the meat was handled correctly.

I don't recommend packing canned meat, like spam and tuna. Besides the initial weight, you have to pack out an empty and odorous can.

The foil packages of tuna and chicken are good sources and contain manageable serving sizes. Be sure to double bag the empty packaging to avoid attracting animals.
Fully cooked meats can still spoil. Bacon is considered a safe product when fully cooked. However it's scent is too strong for bear country, unless you are armed and ready to defend your food.

Cheeses
Block Cheese can be a great addition to a hiker's food bag. Hard cheese is best because it will stay firm and be less likely to escape in your pack. Carry it in a gallon sized ziploc bag, inside you food bag.

When the evening cools off, so will the cheese. Early in the morning, wrap the cold cheese, still in its ziploc bag, in your camp towel or another garment. Bury it in your pack and it will stay cool until the evening.

We carried sharp cheddar this way on 100-degree days.
At lunchtime, you can retrieve it, slice or break off a piece, and roll a tortilla around it.

Cream cheese is excellent on giant bagels, with a cup of hot coffee to wash it down. You can buy it in 8 ounce tubs, enough to cover 6 large bagels. I really loved the strawberry cream cheese on blueberry bagels.

One ounce of block cheese (Colby, cheddar, Swiss) provides: 8 ounces of protein, 10 grams of fat, and 110 calories.

Parmesan cheese improves the evening meal. Sprinkle generously on ramen, rice, potatoes, corn, and meat stews. Besides adding wonderful flavor, a 2 teaspoon serving of Parmesan cheese provides 2 grams of protein, 1.5 grams of fat, 25 calories, and 6% of your daily calcium requirement.

Powdered (dry) Milk

Powdered milk can be added to just about any soup, hot dish or breakfast cereal. Also, you can use it in powdered puddings or for a chocolate shake. Adding a tablespoon of powdered milk to instant coffee smooths out bitterness of some generic brands.

Powdered milk can be purchased ahead of time, in bulk and stored for a long time. Ship yourself a pouch of instant milk in a drop of bounce box. I don't recommend reconstituting it and carrying in water bottles for any length of time. Heat will make it sour quickly and the rim may become difficult to wash.

Stats for milk prove its worth. A third cup provides 8 grams of protein, no fat, 80 calories and 30% of an adult's daily calcium requirements.

Powdered eggs, powdered cheese, protein powders and soy powders can all be incorporated into breakfast beverages, breads and cereals. Availability may be an issue if you don't ship these items in a drop box.

Peanut Butter

Peanut Butter is an all-around favorite for long distance backpackers because it is readily available even in convenience stores, comes in 18 ounce jars and tastes good on a multitude of things, including Snicker's bars. It can be spread on all sorts of tortillas, cookies, crackers, pop tarts, bagels and breads or eaten by the spoonful right out of the jar.

Plain or chunky peanut butter per 2 tablespoons, provides:
protein.... 8 grams
fat...17 grams
calories... 190 grams
iron.... 4% recommended daily requirement

The sugar or carbohydrate content may vary brand to brand. I never empty peanut butter into plastic bags because if it leaks, it could be disastrous. Besides, an empty plastic peanut butter jar makes a great soup or coffee mug. Mine could withstand boiling water. You can solar cook in the empty plastic jar by adding water and ramen noodles and placing it in the sun.

After traversing and crossing Forester Pass, the highest point of the Pacific Crest Trail, Alexa, Cobweb and I pulled out our all-purpose empty peanut butter jars and spoons. We filled each plastic jar with pure snow then added an entire package of instant cocoa powder into each one, mixing well. What delight! Chocolate Ice Cream never tasted so good.

Several peanut butter spreads can be made right on the trail. You can use it straight from the jar as a dip for pretzels or chocolate candy bars. This treat provides some serious calories. Below are some peanut butter mixes I have tried and thoroughly enjoyed.

Chocolate Peanut Butter Spread
1/2 jar peanut butter
1/2 cup chocolate syrup

Gradually stir the syrup into the peanut butter. This tastes great on the spoon, as well as any bread or muffin.

Creamy Frosting and Peanut Butter Spread
1/2 jar of peanut butter
3/4 cup frosting, any flavor
Chopped nuts, optional

Gradually stir the frosting into the jar of peanut butter. Add nuts and mix well. Spread on crackers, bread, or eat by the spoonful.

Peanut Butter and Jelly Spread
1/2 jar peanut butter
3/4-cup jelly or jam

Into the jar of peanut butter, add jelly or jam, bit by bit, stirring well to mix. I choose a jam over a jelly because it will stay thicker even in hot weather.

Peanut Butter-Honey Spread
1/2 jar of peanut butter
1/2-cup honey

Gradually mix honey into peanut butter in the jar. This will be easy to spread, especially in warm weather.

Legumes, Beans and Dried Split Peas
One serving (1/4 cup dried split peas) provides no fat, 110 calories, and 11 grams of protein.

I have found that once finely ground into a powder, legumes only need to soak for 4 hours. Then, bring to a boil, remove from heat and allow to set 10 minutes. Add salt to taste. They are delicious.

You can add ground split peas to various hot dishes.

Another plan is to fully cook the beans at home, then dehydrate and package into Ziploc bags.

Our final resupply on the Colorado Trail taught me just how delectable dehydrated refried beans and tortillas can be. For three nights we had a delightful meal of beans and tortillas. The beans rehydrated fairly quickly in boiling hot water. After feeling spoiled with three regular meals, there were a couple nights of Desperation Soup. The actual formula for Desperation Soup is on page 37.

The following list helps show what a last desperate resupply from a camp store may look like.

From my journal:

The guidebook led us astray here, telling us of the supply of basics this campground store contained. This year, all they had were snack foods, but Rainmaker and I had previously determined to resupply there if at all possible, and save having to hitch into Silverton, and then hitchhiking back. My resupply for 5.5 days was

--11 packages of Grandmas cookies, 2.5 ounces each (to be used for breakfasts, and afternoon break)

--3 bags each cashews, peanuts and beef jerky (for after dinner and pre breakfast snacking, a total of 8 ounces)

--1 Snickers, 5 Milky Way candy bars (lunch desserts)

--6 packages of hot cocoa (running low on coffee)

--4 small packages of assorted chips (lunches, and soup enhancers, for about 16 ounces total)

--about 6 ounces of dehydrated refried beans and 10 tortillas (donated when I told the clerk I would buy any bread off her, this made 3 meals for Rainmaker and I)

--5 snack crackers and 2 snack cookie packages (for a.m snacks)

--Leftovers from previous resupply was 2 ramen seasoning packages, and 2 tablespoons mashed potatoes (to be used for two suppers)
This resupply was the Do-Or-Die type....all I really wanted was to get to Durango without starving to death.

The difficulty we had in hitching into and out of Lake City helped in this decision.
Every day we rose by 6:15 and packed up. Rainmaker did his back warm up exercises, and we headed out. My feet and knees had reoccurring pains, so I tried to take smaller steps. With just one hiking pole, the trail was

taking a greater toll on my joints. Also, last year's AT thru hike had caused some injuries, not totally resolved.

Friday night we camped just 22 miles from the Durango Trailhead, near Taylor Lake. It was peaceful, and the site lovely.

The evening sun warmed the tent, and then the rains started. The next morning, the clouds had thinned and we hiked this one last full day thoughtfully. By 2:30 the rains caught up to us once more, in sheets, drenching us as we looked for a camping spot. The rule seemed to be: If there was water, there was no place to put a tent. If there was a tent spot, the water was nowhere near.

By the time we crossed lower Junction Creek, the two tiny nearby camp spots were flooded and muddy. We kept hiking as evening drew near. It was 7 p.m. and still the rained poured down. I merely followed David, watching his feet, when suddenly he stopped and said, "How about here?" I raised my head to see from under my hood. It was a wide spot in the trail, packed down and level.

"Sure!" I said and we began to raise the tent, but the stakes refused to go in. I bent several and he came over and straightened them until finally the Tacoma stood up, our shelter, large and strong. We crawled in, keeping the wet stuff in our vestibules, glad for the separate double wide doors and full length vestibules. I crawled in, removing my mud caked boots in the process, sliding out of my clothes like a snake sheds its skin, leaving everything behind in the vestibule. Meanwhile Rainmaker was doing the same. It wasn't that bad, now that we were inside the tent, facing warm sleeping bags. My muddy mess was mine alone and wouldn't interfere with his. He had plenty of his own to deal with.

Nuts
Nuts are known to have a lot of fat and protein. Happily, that's just what we are after. If you find digesting them hard while fast hiking or climbing, as I do, you can enjoy them just before bedtime. Addition of calories before bedtime can help one to sleep warmer. One female hiker I met swore they kept her from having to get up to pee in the middle of the night. She explained it gave her body something to do beside fill her bladder.

Digestion problems are characterized by bloating, gas and stomach pain.
Stats for nuts vary, but generally speaking, for every 1/4 cup:
protein.... 8 grams, 17 grams of fat, up to 210 calories, and 4% iron -
recommended daily requirement.

A little fun with the Daily Recommended dosage thing: I mean, would a Brown Bear need
more than one apple to be heart healthy, while a small black bear only require one?

BREADS

Breads are one of the foods I really crave while backpacking. Homemade and fresh out of the oven, who wouldn't dream about slathering some butter over a tender moist slice? Bread is bulky and low in calories, so here are some of my recipes for taking care of that craving back in the wilderness.

I would never have thought of tortillas as a backpacking food when I first got into this lifestyle. Then Rainmaker showed me how good they can be and that they can hold up to the rigors of weeklong hikes.

Rolling a tortilla around a chunk of cheese *(for you ultralighters, who don't carry pocket knives)* or a slice of cheese *(for you survivalists who won't leave home without one)* makes a wonderful treat.

You can smear one with peanut butter or another spread.

You can use a tortilla instead of a spatula (now who carries one of Them?) to wipe out jars of foodstuff and sop up the last drops of gravy. If you lose your spoon or want to go native, a tortilla makes a great substitute for an eating utensil.

Flour tortillas travel well if left flat in the Ziploc bag, and laid over a rounded stuff sack. It's like a papoose riding along, content and warmed by the sunshine.

Rainmaker picked up some Best-If-Eaten-By-6-01-00 Whole Wheat Tortillas on August 6th in a Beldon, California hiker box. It was a very sparse resupply stop so these appeared to be a great find. But, being two months old, neither one of us knew what flavors; critters or flora might have attached themselves to this package of 10.

Finally one night Rainmaker opened the bag of flour tortillas. I concentrated while he took his first bite, monitoring his face for signs of honest pleasure or disgust. Since we cook and resupply autonomously, any minute signal would be important for future trades and negotiations.

Happily, they were as good and pure as the day they were made. Three chocolate Oreo cookies was a fair trade for one best-if-eaten-by-6-01-00-Whole Wheat Tortillas.

Stats on grains used below; per 1/4 cup:
corn...1 gram fat, 2 grams protein, 100 calories
white flour.... 0 grams fat, 3 grams protein, 100 calories
whole wheat flour.... 0.5 grams fat, 4 grams protein, 90 calories

I'm fascinated by old time skills, including baking tortillas from scratch. Tortillas are so cheap, however, that if you like them and don't share this fascination, I suggest you buy them in bulk and repackage them into double serving sizes for backpacking trips.

Authentic Mexican Tortillas
2 cups white flour
3 T. oil
½ tsp. salt
1 T. baking powder
½ c. warm water

Mix Flour, oil, salt and baking powder.
Using your hands, begin to work the water and flour mixture together, kneading well until the dough is pliable and elastic. If it becomes a little sticky, add a bit of oil, not flour, to make handling them easier.

Divide dough into 9 even balls. Roll out each one on a very lightly floured surface, turning and flipping it over to make a nice a circle. Shake off any extra flour before you cook it on a dry, hot skillet.

When the tortilla begins to have little bubbles, flip to other side. Cover with a towel to keep warm and moist. Makes 9 medium tortillas.

Whole Wheat Tortillas
1 ½ cups whole-wheat flour
1 teaspoon salt
1 Tablespoon baking powder
3 Tablespoons oil
½ cup warm water

Mix water, oil, salt and baking powder.
Add the flour, a little at a time, kneading well until dough is soft and elastic. If it becomes a little sticky, add a bit of oil, not flour to facilitate handling.

Divide dough into 6 even balls. Roll out each one as thinly as possible on a very lightly floured surface, turning and flipping it over to make a circle. Shake off any extra flour before you cook it on a dry, hot skillet.

When the tortilla begins to have little bubbles, flip to other side. Cover with a towel to keep warm and moist. Makes 6 medium tortillas.

Corn Tortillas

These tortillas have a great flavor, and hold together better than 100% corn tortillas do.

1 c. self-rising corn meal
1 c. white flour
1/2 tsp. salt
3 T. oil
3/4 cup warm water

Mix the corn meal, flour and salt. Stir in the oil and water.

Mix well with a spoon. Form into small balls, rolling out each one until as thin as possible. Cook on a hot dry griddle until it begins to bubble. Flip and cook other side.

Stack on a plate, and cover with a clean dry towel to keep them moist.

Indian Fried Bread

This recipe I consider a backcountry base camping recipe because of the amount of oil it requires for frying. They are very filling and versatile, however, and a favorite at Powwows and Mountain man Rendezvouses.-

2 Tablespoons baking powder
2 teaspoons sugar
1-teaspoon salt
5 cups flour

Place the baking powder, sugar, salt and flour into a gallon zip lock bag. Shake well to mix.

For every fry bread, measure out 1/4 cup flour mixture. Add enough warm water to moisten the flour and form into a small ball.

Pat until flat with your hands. Poke three to four slits in each one to facilitate frying.

Heat enough oil in your pot to a depth of one inch. Pinch off just a tad of dough to test. If it bubbles and sizzles, it's ready.

Drop prepared fry bread into pot. Fry until puffy and brown on one side. Flip and repeat.

Serve Indian Fried bread with taco fixings or ith cinnamon and sugar for dessert.

Sweet Biscuits
This recipe was born at a youth camp one summer when supplies ran low and we scavenged in the pantry for dry goods. We knew pancake mix was a keeper because it had all the right ingredients. The kids scarfed them up and returned home to request their own moms fix Camp Biscuits

2 Cups complete pancake mix
3 Tablespoons oil
Oil for frying

Measure the mix and oil into a bowl. Add warm water, one tablespoon at a time, until it forms a dough that is stiff enough to handle.
Knead dough until it is smooth and light.
Form into biscuits trailside by hand, or at home with a rolling pin on lightly floured surface, if desired.

Heat oil until a bit of dough dropped in the pan sizzles and rises to the top. Gently drop biscuits in oil, frying each side about 2 minutes. Remove from oil. Drain on paper towel. These biscuits are great with soup and stew. Smear with butter and cheese.

Bear Sign or Chocolate Drop Doughnuts
I don't know if you would call this bread, or dessert, or even an appetizer. Whatever it is, they are very good. I developed this recipe after my sons read a Luis Lamoure book. Sometimes I'll get the question, Why is it called Bear Sign? The answer: if you saw something like this laying on the trail, what might you think left it?
1/2 cup white sugar
1 teaspoon cinnamon
2 tablespoons baking powder
1/4 teaspoon salt
3 tablespoons cocoa
2 cups flour
1/3 cup dry (powdered) milk

extra sugar for rolling
oil or grease for frying (inch deep)

Mix the sugar, cinnamon, baking powder, salt, cocoa, flour and dry milk into a gallon zip lock bag. Shake well to mix.

For every 9 doughnuts, measure 1/2-cup mix into container, with 3-4 Tablespoons warm water.

Heat enough oil in a pan to cover bottom one inch deep. Test oil by dropping a small bit of dough into the hot oil. If it begins to rise to the top and sizzle, it's ready.
Drop dough by teaspoons into hot oil, cooking about 3 minutes. Remove from grease with fork. Immediately place sign onto paper towel. Roll in extra white or powdered sugar.

The whole recipe will make about 32 sign.

Homemade Bagels
   There are so many variations of bagels. They are extra delicious, travel well, are high in protein and make a great sandwich. Making your own bagels is tedious but fun, a great activity for kids and people waiting on the calendar so they can finally go hiking.

2 Tablespoons yeast
1 ½ cup warm water
4 eggs
3 Tablespoons sugar
1 Tablespoon salt
4 ½ cups flour

Dissolve yeast in the warm water in a large bowl.
Mix eggs, sugar, salt and flour. Knead for 2-3 minutes. Let rise for 10 minutes.
Divide into 12 balls and shape into bagels then place them on a greased baking sheet. Cover for 20 minutes and let rise

Fill a kettle with water and bring it to a boil while you pop the whole tray of raised bagels into the oven. Broil one side till golden brown, approximately 1 minute.

Flip and broil other side, 5 inches from heat on top rack.

Your water should be boiling by now. Add 1-tablespoon sugar to the kettle and turn stovetop heat down to maintain just a light boil

Now, gently place three bagels at a time in boiling water, flip once. Do not boil for more than one minute per side or they will become water logged and collapse.
Drain on wire rack and place back on greased sheet. Bake at 375 degrees for 20-25 minutes. Makes 12.

Rye Bagels: substitute 1 cup of rye flour for 1 cup of white flour and add 1-tablespoon garlic while missing in the sugar and salt.

Cinnamon and Raisin: mix into dough 1-tablespoon cinnamon and 1 cup raisins.

Whole Wheat Bagels: Substitute one cup of whole wheat flour for one cup of white flour.

Onion Bagels: Stir one cup finely chopped onions and 1 teaspoon chives into dough.

Chocolate Chip: Mix one cup of chocolate chips into dough.

Nuts and Such Bagels: Mix one cup of finely chopped nuts and 1/2 teaspoon nutmeg into dough.

Yes, absolutely they are a lot of work and you can buy them nearly everywhere, but isn't it cool to know you can make them yourself at home?

Apple Pancakes

1 cup complete pancake mix
1/2 teaspoons cinnamon
1/4 cup brown sugar
a handful of crushed dried apple rings
1/2 cup water
oil

Combine the pancake mix with the cinnamon, brown sugar, dried apples, and water.
Heat oil in your pan until drop of water sizzles on it. Spoon mixture onto pan, flipping to other side when bubbles begin to form.

Serve with honey, jelly, or one of the peanut butter spreads found in the Meat, Cheese and Protein section.

Rainmaker loves his cowboy coffee with blueberry pancakes. I go all out when we're doing a short backpacking trip. Pancake syrup is in the plastic bottle. Caramelized fresh peaches make a great side dish.

Wild Berry Pancakes

Here we take advantage of a premade mix, easy to find in most stores.

1 cup complete pancake mix
1/2 teaspoons cinnamon
1/4 cup brown sugar or white sugar

a handful of rinsed, clean berries
1/2 cup water
oil

Combine the pancake mix with the cinnamon, sugar, berries, and water. Heat some oil in your pan until drop of water sizzles on it. Spoon the mixture into pan. Flip to other side when bubbles begin to form.

Serve with honey, jelly, or one of the peanut butter spreads found in the Meat, Cheese and Protein section.

Whole Wheat Rolls
1 1/2 cups warm water
1 tablespoon yeast
1/4 cup brown sugar
2 teaspoons salt
1 cup white flour
2-3 cups whole wheat flour
1/4 cup margarine

In a large bowl, blend the water, yeast, sugar, salt and white flour. Mix well, and allow to work for 5 minutes.

Gradually stir in the whole wheat flour, mixing well with each additional 1/2 cup. Stir for an additional five minutes to form the gluten. This will make the dough soft and the bread cells smaller.

When dough is somewhat stiff and elastic, cover with clean dry towel, and allow to rise in warm place until doubled.

In a 9x12 inch pan, melt the margarine. Spread margarine to coat the bottom of pan. Place dough in pan, coating on all sides with melted margarine. Pinch off golf ball size pieces of dough, roll until rounded, and lay in pan.
Allow to rise once more.
Bake at 375 degrees, for approximately 12 minutes. Do not over bake because this will cause the rolls to be dry.

This is an exceptional roll to take on the trail, with cheddar cheese sliced for lunch and snacks.

Quick Yeast Muffins
---a very fast and easy muffin to make ahead, for trail adventures

1 cup warm water
1 tablespoon yeast
1/4 cup brown sugar
3/4 teaspoons salt
1 cup white flour
1 cup whole wheat flour
1/4 cup margarine
In a large bowl, blend the water, yeast, sugar, salt and white flour. Mix well, and allow to work for 5 minutes.

Gradually stir in the whole wheat flour, mixing well with each additional 1/2 cup. Continue to stir for an additional five minutes to create a somewhat stiff and elastic batter.
Next, spoon into greased muffin tins. Allow to rise in warm place until doubled.

Bake at 375 degrees until lightly browned, about 12 minutes depending on muffin size.

Roasted Fresh Bread
---fresh yeast bread you can make over a campfire

1 Tablespoon white sugar
1 Tablespoon dry yeast
2 teaspoons salt
2 1/2 cups white flour
2 Tablespoon oil (reserve for later)

Measure all dry ingredients into a gallon size Ziploc bag. Shake to blend.

Build a good campfire, and allow it to burn down to hot coals. Measure 3/4 cup of warm water and two tablespoons oil into the ziploc bag with dry ingredients. It should be stiff enough to handle.

Knead well by squeezing the bag and allow to rest for 20 minutes.

Remove walnut size pieces of dough from the bag and form long flattened shapes. Wrap each portion of dough around a roasting stick lengthwise.

Roast slowly over campfire, turning to brown as you would a marshmallow.
For smaller groups, simply cut the recipe in half, or portion dry ingredients as needed into cup with warm water. Proceed with directions.

My family loved to go car camping. Part of the attraction was the Roasting of Food Stuff over the campfire. Besides hot dogs, marshmallows and apples, we came up with the fresh bread. Anything on a stick that a youngster can manage by themselves is ideal camp food, in my opinion.

Focaccia Italian Bread

I learned how to make Focaccia while I was working in the Grand Tetons. It's an Italian Herb Bread. Our bake shop recipe made a sticky dough, which was then placed in a deep sheet pan where olive oil had been drizzled.
Or, maybe I should say, dumped.

Then the mass is allowed to "proof" which means rise in regular home cooking lingo.
This bubbly dough is then topped with a garnish like rosemary sprigs, red pepper flakes, or parsley, some kosher salt or sea salt and baked at 375 for about 20 minutes.

As a variation, you can top it with cinnamon and sugar, even toasted nuts or coconut. This coffee cake type bread is great for breakfast.

It's fantastically easy gourmet bread, packed with calories from the olive oil. Make it before heading out to the trail.

Here's the basic recipe:
2.5 cups of warm water
1 Tablespoon dry yeast
2 Tablespoons sugar
1/2 Tablespoon regular salt
4 1/4 cup flour

Stir this batter together until well blended, then an additional five minutes to develop the gluten. Next, add ½ teaspoons of two to five spices of your choice. We used rosemary, sage, onion salt, garlic salt and thyme. One of my daughters didn't have the rosemary on hand so we used basil instead. After all, it's Italian bread. It turned out great.

Now, with the batter well mixed, and heavily spiced, dump a generous amount of olive or canola oil in a sheet pan or 9 x 13. There should be enough to actually pool a bit. Make sure the pan is coated.

Now, scrape the batter into the pan. Set in a warm place and allow to double in size, at the very least. You should see yeasty bubbles forming.

Now, sprinkle the kosher salt and garnish on top. Dip your fingertips in oil and make "dimples" by lightly touching the top of the dough. Bake in hot oven, see above, until lightly browned.

This bread can be served in so many ways, as a sandwich, side dish with marinara, with grilled steaks and salad for a complete meal, or eaten for breakfast. All have been done this very week.

You can vary the spices; make it plain, or with chili theme. Have fun, it's a cheap food and one I'll do on the trail with my ultralight soda can baking system.

Photo of the blue mountains in North East Georgia. These views are what keeps me backpacking.

Finishing a hot meal with something sweet is natural. Maybe its because Americans eat more than one hundred and fifty pounds of sugar, on average, each year. Some of that sugar is from soda and processed foods. It's hard to deny the sweet tooth. A candy bar, a handful of M&Ms or maybe some dried fruit is simple enough. But if you want a little something special or something different you didn't just eat at lunch time, here are some easy recipes.

Chinese Clusters
12 ounce bag of butterscotch chips
4 cups Chow Mein noodles
waxed paper

Melt butterscotch chips in microwaveable bowl for 2 minutes. Or you can melt them over low heat in a saucepan, stirring constantly.

If you are making these candies on the trail, fill your pot half full with butterscotch chips, and melt slowly over low heat.
Then, stir in the chow Mein noodles. If your pot isn't very big, you might only have enough room to use 2 cups of noodles. The mixture should be moist, and all the noodles well covered so that when the chips hardened, the noodles stick together.

Drop small mounds, using a spoon onto waxed paper. Allow to set until hardened. Place in a Ziploc bag.

These travel very well, if you can keep from devouring them beforehand.

A really basic trick I learned is to place the butterscotch chips and noodles in a Ziploc bag and shake to mix. Set it in the sun until the chips melt. During the night it will cool and solidify. Then you can break it into chunks and eat.

Use this solar melting and mixing trick for the next two recipes as well while you're on the trail. With hardly any effort, you can have some really nice treats by nightfall.

White Chocolate Confetti
One 12 ounce bag mini pretzels
5 cups Cheerios
5 cups Chex
2 cups salted peanuts
1 pound M&Ms
In a large bowls mix the pretzels, cereals, peanuts and m&ms. Set aside.

Melt together in a saucepan:
Two 12 ounce bags of white chocolate chips
3 Tablespoons butter

Pour the melted chips over the dry ingredients.
Spoon onto waxed paper. Allow to set until hardened. Break into pieces.
Store in a Ziploc bag.

Rice Crispy Candies
12 ounce bag of chocolate chips
2 cups Rice Crispies
½ cup salted chopped nuts
½ cup raisins

Melt chocolate chips over gentle heat, or in a microwave. Stir in the nuts and raisins. Add rice Crispies. Drop by teaspoons onto wax paper. Allow to set until firm. They travel well.

Peanut Butter is a staple in a backpacker's food list. Unless you're allergic to nuts, use this high protein, readily available food to make desserts. I know of several ways to make peanut butter balls, all of them delicious. Use the first one at home. It requires more ingredients and effort.

Peanut Butter Balls
The first version
2 cups crushed graham crackers
2 cups peanut butter
2 cups powdered sugar
4 tablespoons butter
8 ounces Dipping chocolate

Combine graham crackers, peanut butter, powdered sugar and butter. Form into balls, and dip into melted dipping chocolate. Place on wax paper. When firm, place in ziploc bags. Store in cool place.

Peanut Butter Balls
The second version
2 cups powdered milk
2 cups peanut butter
1/2 cup honey
8 ounces Dipping chocolate

Combine milk powder, peanut butter, and honey. Form into balls, and chill for 2 hours.
Dip into melted dipping chocolate. Place on wax paper. When firm, place in ziploc bags.
Store in cool place.

Basic Trail Peanut Butter Balls
Of course, you can make and eat peanut butter balls without dipping them in chocolate.

If you need an empty plastic jar while on the trail for solar cooking and making snow-ice cream, buy some peanut butter and, use the peanut butter to make these treats.

Mix peanut butter with crumbled Oreo cookies, animal crackers or powdered milk. Add chocolate chips, and sweetener, like sugar or honey. Make the dough stiff so you can form them into balls.
These make very high calorie snacks. You can utilize crumbs you might have in that sack of Trail Mix, too, just be careful the crumbs are not too salty. Very delicious.

It's nice to take it easy on the trail, whenever you can, whenever you're not trying to make it to the post office before it closes. I did this sketch while working at the Georgia Heritage Center, a local gallery of demonstrating artists.

Better to have loafed and lost than never to have loafed at all

Double Dipped Grahams
---makes a wonderful dessert, so easy even kids can help you make them.

Box of graham crackers
peanut butter, smooth or chunky style or
 you can switch it up by using cream cheese
two flavors- white almond, butterscotch, or chocolate dipping chocolate
wax paper

Break crackers into quarters.
Spread peanut butter or cream cheese on one side, top with another cracker. Set aside.

In a microwaveable bowl, or saucepan, slowly melt one flavor dipping chocolate. Dip prepared graham cookies into chocolate, coating as much of the cookie as possible. Lay on wax paper and allow to fully dry.

If you are doing this in camp or trail side, you may choose to lick out the pan between flavors.

Melt the second flavor of dipping chocolate, and dip every graham cookie in this second coating. You will have two colors visible.

Allow to set until totally cooled and the chocolates are dry to touch. Store in ziploc baggies or containers with tight fitting lid. These travel well, and have lots of energy and calories.

Blonde Brownies

1 yellow cake mix (18 ounce box)
2 eggs
1/3 cup oil
1/2 cup brown sugar

Into a medium sized mixing bowl combine the ingredients in order given. Grease and flour a 9x13 pan. Spread evenly into pan. Bake at 375 degrees for 15 minutes.

Especially good frosted with Easy Chocolate Peanut butter Frosting, directions on page 73.

Five Layer Bars

6 Tablespoons margarine
1 cup graham cracker crumbs
1 cup flake coconut
1 cup chocolate chips
1 cup chopped nuts
1 can (15 ounces) sweetened condensed milk

Melt margarine in a 9x9 inch pan. Sprinkle graham crackers over it, followed by coconut, chocolate chips, and the nuts. Pour the canned milk over the last layer.
Bake at 350 degrees for about 30 minutes. Cut into squares while still slightly warm.

If you are taking these out on the trail, or shipping them in a bounce box, let the squares cool completely, then wrap each square individually in plastic wrap.

Rocky Road Candy
This one really lends itself to ziploc on trail preparation. Simply put all the ingredients into a gallon bag, allow to melt in the sun, then set in the shade to cool. Break into bits. Voila!

1 bag semi-sweet chocolate chips
1/2 bag colored or plain miniature marshmallows
1/3 cup chopped pecans

Melt chocolate slowly in a saucepan or microwave. Stir in marshmallows and pecans. With a tablespoon, drop onto waxed paper and form into a log. Chill for 2 hours. Cut into 1/2 inch pieces.

Oh Henry Bars
1 cup brown sugar
1/2 cup white sugar
2 sticks margarine
4 cups oatmeal
1 cup peanut butter
1 cup chocolate chips

Mix the sugars, margarine and oatmeal. Place in 11x15 greased baking sheet. Bake at 350 degrees for 13 minutes, or until golden.

Remove from oven and top with chips and peanut butter by quickly distributing chocolate chips over bars along with spoonfuls of the peanut butter. Place back in oven for three minutes.

Remove from oven and spread the melted chips and peanut butter evenly. Allow to cool before cutting.

Cut and wrap individually for the trail.

Carmel Chocolate Bars
1 chocolate cake mix
1/3 cup evaporated milk
1 stick margarine

Stir the cake mix, milk, and melted butter together. Grease a 9x13 pan. Pat batter into pan, reserving 1/3 cup for later. Bake in preheated 350 degree oven for 6 minutes.

Remove and spread:
1 cup chocolate chips
1 cup pecans

Melt in a sauce pan:
14 ounces caramel candy
1/3 cup evaporated milk
Pour this over cake now. Spoon reserved cake batter over this and
continue baking at 350 degrees, for 20 minutes.

Peanut Butter Cookies
Rainmaker needed an empty 18 ounce peanut butter plastic jar at
home. These 4 dozen cookies were the result.
2 sticks margarine (1 cup)
1 cup brown sugar
1 cup white sugar
2 eggs
1 1/2 cups peanut butter
4 cups self-rising flour

Cream the butter and sugars together. Add eggs and peanut butter. Blend
well. Stir in flour.
Roll into balls. Place on ungreased cookie sheet and bake at 375 degrees
for 12 minutes or until golden brown. Remove and allow to cool.

Easy Chocolate-Peanut butter Frosting
Use this frosting to increase protein and calorie count. It's easy to top
any pan of bars, right out of the oven

12 ounce bag of chocolate chips
6 Tablespoons creamy peanut butter

Remove hot pan of bars from oven. Turn off the oven. Pour chocolate chips
evenly over bars, spoon peanut butter on top as well. Don't worry about
spreading it yet.
Place pan back in oven. Wait 3 minutes.
Remove from oven. Use a butter knife to spread melted chocolate chips and
peanut butter together, covering bars evenly. This frosting will set up
nicely, and not be sticky, allowing you to pack them easily.

A 12 ounce bag of chocolate chips adds 1760 calories, 99 grams of fat. With the peanut butter's additional 360 calories, and 34 grams of fat, this frosting will add 2120 calories, and 133 grams of fat, to every 9x13 pan of bars. If you cut them into 15 pieces, (3x2.5 inches) you have increased your calories available by 141.3, and fat by 8.86 grams. This is important for long distance hikers.

Kitchen storage containers don't have to cost money. From left to right back row: a protein powder container makes a flour canister, a soda bottle becomes a water bottle. A cocoa powder container is stackable and has a tight lid.

Front row: glass salsa jar holds dehydrated orange peel while a glass mushroom jar holds coffee beans.

A dehydrator allows you the freedom to take with you all sorts of interesting, healthy and exotic foods. You can add spices to fresh fruits, then dry them as they come into season. Take advantage of sales and bountiful harvests.

Properly dehydrated foods can be kept a long time. Freeze or store in the refrigerator if your home is warm and humid, however, just to be sure no mold develops.

Our dehydrator has four racks, one sauce tray (a solid plastic tray that allows you to make fruit leather, cheese leather, chili sauces and more) and one mesh plastic tray for smaller foods like peas.

Ours also has a blower with different heat settings. I have used a passive heat dehydrator which relies on heat rising to circulate the air. With this method, you must be more careful to spread the food out and rotate the trays from top to bottom every 4 hours. It will take longer using the passive heat to dehydrate your product, so be extremely careful to spread sauces thinly.

I found that one sauce tray was not enough for all my projects requiring multiple trays of product, so I bought a package of disposable aluminum pizza pans. I used the original plastic sauce tray as a pattern by laying it on top and tracing around it with a black magic marker. Then I cut the circle out. Lastly I cut out a hole in the center of each pan. They fit perfectly and had a nice ridge along the circumference which kept the sauces where they were put.

Remember to lightly spray these sauce trays with a non-stick pan spray before spreading the food on top. This will greatly simplify removing the leathers.

Cranberry Sauce

One gallon cranberry sauce will make several sandwich bags of cranberry leather. It tastes like jelly and is especially good on warmed up tortillas.

Lightly spray the sauce trays for your dehydrator. Drain excess liquid found on the top of the cranberry sauce. Slice off thin pieces of cranberry sauce and lay on the trays. Turn your dehydrator to full heat.

When the leathers are dry enough to handle, turn each piece over to finish drying. When finished, the fruit leathers will be chewy due to the high sugar content. Place in containers, and store in freezer.

Fruit leathers are great to eat just as they are. You can also eat them with bread and rolls. Use fruit leather to make pemmican. You'll find a recipe for Pemmican in the chapter entitled **Everything Except**.

Sometimes you'll have various items in the process of dehydrating, in different stages. Perhaps banana chips are almost done, cranberry sauce is on two trays, and the fourth tray has a marinated beef jerky.

This works fine as long as you do not allow any meat juices to drip onto fruits or vegetables. Meats must be dried quickly.

Remember not to prepare them on the same cutting board you use for preparing fruits and vegetables. If you must use the same board, turn it upside down, or scrub it and sterilize it with a drop of cholrine in half cup of water. Rinse the board well before proceeding with your food preparations.

Safe food handling now will save you trouble on the trail.

Cheese Sauce
I happened upon this cheese sauce when the hospital I was working for sold off its inventory of Y2K product. Its better to buy the cheese powder if you get it.
Open one gallon of cheese sauce. Spread evenly over *dry, unsprayed* sauce trays. Dry on high setting. When it is dry enough to handle, turn pieces over, and continue dehydrating. With a paper towel, sponge off any excess fat that may separate from the product. These cheese leathers make wonderful snacks and additions to hot meals.

Tomato Sauce
Spray sauce trays and spread product evenly. Add spices, like garlic, basil, salt and pepper or use a basic spaghetti sauce instead. When completely dry, store in plastic bags. Use tomato leather to turn plain rice or pasta into something extraordinary.

Dehydrating fruits is very easy. If you have ever had homemade banana chips, or dried apples you will probably agree that they are far tastier than the products sold in stores.

An important key to delicious dried fruits is to have ripe fruit to start with. Some grocery stores mark down "past prime" fruit. This is the time to bring out the dehydrator and take advantage of the sale. Buy in bulk, at least five to ten pounds of fruit at once, to make the process worth your time. And, even if it looks clean, always wash fruit before slicing it.

Some health authorities recommend a prewash of a 10 parts per million chlorine and water spray before washing. This is about one drop of chlorine per quart of water. If you chose to use the spray, rinse well, and pat dry.

Fresh or canned peaches, canned pineapple, mandarin oranges, and cherries are excellent also. Drain the juice and use it to make jello. Let the fruit settle and air dry a few minutes before arranging on trays.

Dried Bananas or Banana Chips

Start with as many ripe bananas you can get. Bananas are best dried when they have brown freckles on them showing they are ripe and sweet.

Peel and slice ripe but firm bananas to about 1/4 inch thickness, directly onto the dehydrator trays. If your dehydrator has settings, choose the fruit temperature. If yours doesn't have a control dial, don't worry. They will still be fine.

Place banana slices close together, but not over lapping. After about 4 hours, rotate trays so that the bottom tray is now on the top. Once the slices shrink noticeably, you can consolidate the banana chips onto one or two trays, and fill the emptied trays with more fresh slices. Allow to dry until they are almost brittle. We like ours just a little chewy, and bag them at that stage. For safest long term storage, put in Ziploc bags and store in the freezer.

Dried Apple Discs

Dried Apples are a definite treat anywhere, but especially while hiking when fresh fruit is hard to carry. With no additives, preservatives or artificial colorings, they are extremely healthy.

Gala apples make the best dried apples I have ever tasted. They are very sweet and firm. Also, they don't turn as brown as other varieties. Granny Smith is a tart green apple. It makes a nice addition to a variety pack because the color is so vibrant.

Red Delicious apples tend to lack flavor while Golden Delicious, if fully ripe, are very sweet.

If you use Macintosh, be sure to catch them before they turn mealy. Any variety will do, and actually the bottom line is cost and availability of the apples you are working with.

Start with ripe, firm apples. Avoid soft mushy or grainy apples. They will not slice well. Wash, and dry. I don't peel or core my apples, but like to slice them starting from the stem and working down. This will make a nice star pattern in the apple ring. As they dry the seeds will fall out.

Slice apples to 1/4 inch thickness. Some people garnish with a cinnamon and sugar mixture, others might use a cherry gelatin powder to enhance the flavor before placing them on the trays.

Place apple discs on trays, close together. You may overlap them just on the edges. They will soon shrink.

After about 4 hours, rotate trays. Depending on your dehydrator and the amount of fruit you have in it, it may take between 8 to 24 hours to complete.
Use moderate to low heat to dehydrate the apples within one day. I found the longer they dehydrate, the crisper they become until nearly the texture of potato chips.

Remove, and allow to completely cool before bagging for storage. Apples will become crisp as they cool.

Oranges
---Oranges are beautiful dehydrated. They are translucent, and full of vitamins. The tangy fresh taste is very welcome on the trail

Wash and dry oranges. The seeds will fall out when you slice them, so that is not an important consideration when choosing a variety.
Slice whole oranges 1/8 inch thick into discs, and place on dehydrator trays. Use the fruit and vegetable setting if you have one, about 130 degrees. Dehydrate until crisp and translucent. The peels are very good also. There is no need to discard them.

One winter I craved orange peels. It didn't make any sense. I was not on the trail and could eat anything I wanted. For some reason, the peels from navel oranges just spoke to me. I've learned over the years that if your body craves something, you should eat it.

One exception is plain white sugar. Studies have shown that if you are craving sugar, it could be that you are dehydrated. Drink a full glass of water, then another, and see if that doesn't quench the craving.

At home I dry the orange peel in the gas oven. The pilot light does all the work. I googled "Vitamin C in orange peels" and found this information:

"Orange Peel is one of the greatest sources of vitamin C on earth and should not be left out of your diet as a natural and potent way to enhance your immune system and ward off invasive infection. It is an old and reliable digestive, but important new research has demonstrated promising antioxidant activity."

That's good enough for me. As a natural source of vitamin C, the whole orange is useable and an excellent resource. Once it is dried the peel is somewhat leathery which makes it a good trail treat. It takes a while to chew, but provides a satisfying change to Ramen and oatmeal.

Canned Fruit Compote
Slice any fruits which are in halves, like peaches or pears.
Combine all the canned fruits that have been well drained in a large bowl, stir to mix the flavors.

Next, spread the mixed fruit evenly over dehydrator trays which have been lightly sprayed with a non-stick pan spray.

Using the fruit setting, allow to dry for 4-8 hours, or until no moisture can be felt.
Place in ziploc bags. Makes a tasty addition to any hot cereal in the morning.

Fruit Leather
Various blends of fruits will work well for this delicious trail snack. Its healthy and a good way to use ripe fruit. Anything you could put in a smoothie can go in fruit leather blend.

Bananas, cranberry sauce and applesauce make a great base for fruit leather. Oranges have a lot of liquid in proportion to pulp so they should be combined with bananas. Oranges should not be used alone for leather. Fresh or thawed, frozen fruits may be blended together. Canned fruits should be drained before blending in preparation for making leather.

Wash fruits which won't be peeled, like apples, pears, and plumbs. Remove stones from peaches and plumbs. Peel bananas and melons. Peel oranges if you like.

Now, combine fruits and process in blender. It's easier to do several small batches rather than one that huge one. Blend everything at medium speed until pureed. Repeat as necessary until all fruit is ready.

Spray the sauce trays with a non-sticking pan spray. Pour the pureed fruit onto the trays until it is about 3/8 inch thick. Dry at 130-140 degrees until it feels leathery, approximately 6 hours. Remove while still warm, rolling it up as you go. If the leather is done, you should feel any stickiness, or dampness in your product.

Store in a cool dry place. For longer periods, store in refrigerator or freezer.

Chili

Oils and fats do not dehydrate because the oils will not evaporate. Keeping this in mind, if you wish to dehydrate canned, store bought chili, look for a brand that has very little fat in its contents. Read the label to check the ingredients.

I tried using a store brand which had meat in it. The oils and fats were visible, and even after removing the solidified pieces, the remaining fat continued to delay the dehydrating process. Oil had to be poured off later.

I'm not trying to reduce fat or calories in hiker recipes. These high density calories are necessary on a long hike, providing energy and body fuel for sleeping warm. However, fat impedes progress in the dehydrating process.

I look for a brand that is meatless or low fat. Once processed, I'll add more dehydrated, cooked ground beef later.

The method: Pour chili onto sauce trays to 1/4 inch thickness. With the heat setting on high, dehydrate until crumbly and totally dry. Allow to cool completely before storing in Ziploc bags.

If you'd rather make your own chili, use as much tomato sauce, spices and beans as the recipe calls for. Any meats should be well cooked, broken into small pieces and all fat drained off before adding to the stock. You will want to dehydrate this quickly, so spread thinly on sauce trays, 1/4 inch thick, with heat set on maximum.`

When totally dry and crumbly, allow to cool and store in Ziploc bags. Chili makes a wonderful addition to any casserole bases of pasta, rice, cornmeal and potatoes.

Scalloped Potatoes

Dehydrate leftover scalloped potatoes by spreading the food on sauce trays 1/4 inch thick. Be sure any ham in the potatoes is cut into small pieces. Using the highest setting, dry until crumbly and there is no apparent moisture. Store in zip lock bags. To rehydrate, place one cup of water in your pan, stir in 1 cup of potatoes, and cook until tender.

Beef Stew

This can be an ongoing process. Dehydrate leftover vegetables from supper and put them in a plastic storage container until you have enough to package for single serving meals. Deboned beef, turkey, pork roast or chicken make great additions to the mix.

Be sure all foods are well cooked and sliced thinly or cut into bite size pieces. Place on sauce tray 1/4 inch thick.
Using the highest setting you have, dry until crumbly and no moisture is evident. Store in a Ziploc bag.

As you prepare the mix, add two tablespoons of flour and one teaspoon of bouillon powder, along with parsley flakes, dried minced onion (from the spice rack) and a dash of garlic power.

Adding the spices in the mix makes cooking on the trail much easier. If you like to cook in the pouch, make sure your quart size ziploc bags can take boiling water.

Jerky

Almost any meat can be used to make jerky. However, from experience I would advise No Liver! The thought process that hoaxed me into such folly follows: one, liver is high in iron and b vitamins. Two, liver isn't very palatable in its present form. Three, liver has no fat to trim off, it's pure protein. Four, what have you got to lose?

I began this experiment by slicing half a pound of beef liver into thin strips, then marinating the strips in a soy sauce, smoke flavoring concoction. I mixed everything in a bowl, then wrapped it with plastic and it in the fridge overnight.

The next afternoon, I carefully removed each strip from the marinade and arranged them on several dehydrator trays and plugged in the machine.

For two days, a strange aroma, better described as an odor, permeated the house. I rotated the trays, wondering why it was taking so long to dry. Finally, I had to test it. I pried a piece from the plastic tray and put it in my mouth. Not good, not satisfying, not anything I had anticipated. In fact, I discovered it was as chewy as bubble gum and almost impossible to remove from my teeth. God knows I tried. It was one of the worst things I have ever done in the culinary field. I read later that anything with much cholesterol as liver has, does not belong in the human body. I googled "how much fat does liver have" and found out that although there is no marbling, each serving has 7 grams of fat. No wonder it wouldn't dehydrate!

Rattle Snake, however, dehydrates nicely. I am not advocating the wholesale slaughter of such creatures, but if one should happen your way, then perhaps this recipe will come in handy.

One fine spring afternoon, I went out on the back porch to sew. The screened in, wooden floored area was light and airy, with a nice table, so I kept my machine out there, ready to go at a moment's notice.

As I stepped up to the table, I heard a loud buzzing. It seemed like a motor running wild. I didn't even know what it was, having grown up in Wisconsin. I called out "David, something is wrong out here." I though somehow the motor on my sewing machine had gone wild.

Our black lab stood outside the screen, peering underneath the deck of the porch. Instantly David knew what it was. "A rattler!" He went back inside, put on his snake guards, and picked up his loaded shot gun.

But the snake wasn't moving. He had no intention of leaving his cozy spot in the dirt and leaves, safely snugged 7 feet away from the dog or human revenge.
Fine, Rainmaker thought, and went inside, soon returning with a bucket of hot water. Slowly he poured it through the narrow crack in the floor, right onto that snake.
The buzzing stopped. We waited. The lab moved a few feet, his eyes still glued to the snake. I looked at Rainmaker and asked, "What should I do?"

"Keep an eye out," he replied, and went inside for more water. He returned amid deathly silence. By watching the dog, we could only guess the snake had moved a few feet towards the east. Rainmaker poured water over that spot, and left for more.

Suddenly my eyes were drawn to movement alongside the house. The snake was easing along the leaves, noiseless as the grim reaper.
David had managed to roust this huge rattler out from beneath the back porch. I ran inside, said, "He's tiptoeing out along the house!"

83

Rainmaker's jaw had that set of deadly determination as he picked up the shotgun, stepped outside and faced the snake. Bamm! Two Bamms! The snakes head was blown off. Without wasting any time, he chopped the head off with the blade of a shovel and buried the head, explaining that people have been bitten and died from being bit by a decapitated snake.

For half an hour, the snake coiled tightly, raised its headless body preparing to strike. It seemed to know where David was as he circled the snake, now rattling its warning. I felt like I was in a horror movie. The nerves were still in action, although the brain was 10 inches under the ground, 9 feet away. I felt some pity for the snake, but we both knew he had to kill it or take the risk of this viper making a home there and striking us someday as we hung out the wash on the clothesline.

At last, the creature relaxed, fell quiet, lay out on the ground. Rainmaker and I made a bargain. If he would skin it, I would dry the hide and make jerky. Deal.

Now, anytime some animal threatens me I just say, "The last creature that messed with me ended up jerked and in a Ziploc bag." It's sort of a mantra, like a confidence builder.

How This Recipe Came To Be
In Rainmaker's words:

Before I go any further, let me emphasize that I would never kill any animal unnecessarily. Okay; I do trout fish occasionally, and I'm not swearing off turkey hunting, either. However, when hiking, I do not harm any animal in the wild, and I'm very content to share my property with any critters not exhibiting hostile intent. However, I draw the line at poisonous snakes in the yard and driveway; they have to go.

One early June morning, Brawny had her sewing machine set up on our back porch when we heard a strange buzzing noise. At first, we thought it was from her sewing machine but when she stopped sewing, the buzzing kept going. It took me a few seconds, and then I realized that it was a large rattlesnake directly under the floor. The boards on the porch floor are separated slightly to allow for drainage, so I managed to "coax" the snake to leave by pouring hot water between the boards. When I had a clear shot, I killed it with a shotgun. Believe me, it didn't suffer.

The snake was just under 3 feet long, and had 12 rattles. After severing and burying the head and removing the rattles and skin (I'm getting a hatband, and Brawny is opting for a bracelet), we were left wondering what to do with the rest of it.

---Rainmaker

Appalachian Rattlesnake Jerky

One mature rattlesnake
1 tablespoon soy sauce
1 teaspoon packed brown sugar
1 dash garlic powder

Take one large, mature, dead rattlesnake. Discard head and rattles. Skin, remove innards, and wash well. Using a sharp hatchet, chop into 3 inch lengths. Place in a quart sauce pan, cover with water, and bring to a boil. Continue cooking for two hours, replacing liquid as necessary.

Do not worry about it getting tender. These never do. Remove from stove, discard liquid and allow to cool.

Using a sharp paring knife, gently scrape from the backbone outward to remove meat. Most of the flesh will be found along the spine in thin strips. Take care to avoid the hundreds of tiny rib bones.

Place meat in cereal bowl. Add soy sauce, brown sugar, and garlic powder. Mix well, allow to marinate for 15 minutes.

Place snake meat on "liquid" tray of dehydrator. This is the insert that has no holes. Use the "Meat" setting (145 degrees). It takes about 4 hours to completely dry.

Yield: Approximately one ounce

Jerky Marinade
This marinade may be used for beef, pork, venison, and poultry.

Several pounds of fresh meat
1 cup soy sauce
4 Tablespoons liquid smoke
1/4 cup brown sugar
1/2 teaspoon garlic salt
black pepper, if desired

In a small bowl blend the soy sauce, liquid smoke and brown sugar and garlic salt. Set aside.

Slice meat into strips, trimming off all visible fat. If you work with slightly frozen product, it is easier to slice. Use a sharp knife to facilitate this process.

Place meat strips in a bowl and add marinade. Allow to thaw completely, and assimilate flavors for at least 8 hours in the refrigerator.

Pour meat into a colander and drain juices. Place on dehydrator racks, allowing plenty of room. Do not overlap the pieces. Sprinkle with black pepper if you desire. Set dehydrator on highest temperature.

Allow to dry completely, approximately 8 hours. When it is totally dry, remove racks and allow jerky to cool. Place jerky in a Ziploc bag. If storing for longer periods of time you can keep it in the refrigerator or freezer.

Meats for the casserole
All meat is considered a potential health risk if not handled properly. Always choose fresh or frozen product to start with. The general rule is to never allow meat to sit at temperatures between 40 degrees to 135 degrees for any length of time. Four hours total is considered the cut off point for food safety.

Always wash your hands before and after working with meat. Do not prep any fruits or vegetables with the same equipment without washing first. Keep tasks separate according to types of food product. Work with raw. Sanitize, then work with cooked.

The surface you use should be disinfected also before and after, to avoid possible food contamination. If you choose to marinade raw meats, marinade in the refrigerator. Chose marinades for meat which have high salt content, like soy sauce or teriyaki sauce.

Use the highest heat setting on your dehydrator, and do not overlap the pieces.

Cook all meats to be used in trail casseroles before slicing, dicing or shredding for dehydrating. Canned tuna and canned chicken are exceptions. They only need to be well drained. Choose canned meats that are packed in water not oil.

To dehydrate cooked or drained canned meats, place on trays, spacing evenly. Rotate trays every three to four hours. When completely dried, allow to cool. Store in Ziploc bags in the freezer or refrigerator.

You can add dried meats to any hot meals of cornmeal, pasta, rice or potatoes. Just put a couple tablespoons of this dried meat in the pot at the beginning of the cooking process trailside.

Vegetables

Most vegetables should be dehydrated after first cooking them. Having practiced on raw carrots, onions and peas, I soon realized the truth of the matter. Raw, dehydrated vegetables will not rehydrate in my lifetime or yours. They just change from hard dry vegetables to hard wet ones, becoming chewy after a long time simmering.

To facilitate cooking soups and stews on the trail, please be sure to start with steamed, boiled or baked vegetables. A few exceptions follow.

Sweet Potato Slices
Peel and slice as thinly as possible firm, raw, sweet potatoes. Lay them closely together on trays. Dehydrate until crispy. Eat as a raw food, like potato chips.

Tomatoes
Wash and dry fully ripe, but not mushy tomatoes. Slice to 1/2 inch thick. Place on dehydrator tray. Using the highest setting, allow to dry

completely. When cool, remove and store in Ziploc bags. May be broken up into bits later, and added to pasta, rice, or lentils.

The saying goes, a bad day on the trail is better than the best day at work. This pen and ink sketch brings back fond memories of all the free spirited hikers I've met in my journeys.

EVERYTHING EXCEPT

Sometimes all you need is a little something to make an ordinary meal delicious: a little pinch of salt, a sprinkling of cinnamon, dash of sugar, a teaspoon of butter buds, a squirt of olive oil.

Below is a list of additives you could consider bringing along, and ways of utilizing them to the maximum. You can find tiny plastic bags in the craft section of large department stores.

Salt:
It is amazing what a dash of salt can do for food. Bring along a tiny plastic bag with a few tablespoons of salt and you may be surprised how it can enhance your food. A pinch of salt in cooked grains, on fresh fruit, in casseroles and desserts can make a huge difference.

White Sugar:
White sugar in individual packages are available everywhere. Be sure to place them in a good Ziploc bag to avoid ants.

Brown Sugar:
This can be added to breakfast cereals, and even eaten as candy. A small bit in your mouth after supper can substitute for dessert if you are running low on food. Mix with catsup for a bar-b-que sauce.

Butter Buds
This item is a little hard to find, so stock up when you can. This flavoring is sold in boxes with 8 small packages inside. Look for them in the cooking isle. Butter buds make creamed casseroles, noodles, hot cereals and breads taste wonderful. Sprinkle liberally on your food, or mix with a tablespoon hot water to make a spread.

Oil
Use olive oil in everything from oatmeal to soups for that silky texture and extra calories. Carry canola oil, olive oil or vegetable oil in a tightly sealed bottle designed for liquids. Test the seal to be sure it doesn't leak and keep it in an outside pocket or inside your cook set. Olive oil packs the most flavor.

Cinnamon:
This can be added directly at home to mixes, or brought in a small plastic shaker. Add a dash or two of nutmeg for a really spicy flavor from home. Cinnamon has health benefits as well.

Garlic Salt or Garlic Powder:
Great with any hot supper dish, garlic can be added to dumpling mixes, and hot roasted breads. Use in instant mashed potatoes to make them more interesting.

Instant Potatoes:
This product is great for thickening the broth in ramen noodles, stews and other hot dishes. It makes meals more filling. Adding just a tablespoon of instant potatoes to soup makes it easier to eat with a small trail spoon.

Pickle Relish:
I carry the individual packages when I can find them. A little relish, tastes great on onion or garlic bagels.

Salsa:
Salsa is easy to find in nearly every fast food establishment. Be sure you don't get stuff hotter than you are used to. It's great on tortillas with cheese or in rehydrated chili. Use a package to add zing to Ramen noodles.

Black Pepper:
Black pepper is especially good on beef and chicken. Add a pinch to stew and chili. Spice up Ramen or veggie burgers.

Pemmican
I'm fascinated by Native American and mountain man skills. They carried pemmican on long journeys because of its high calorie content and sustainability. This recipe is just one of many. Switch up the ingredients according to availability. Use any fruit leather, dried fruits or jerky that you have to make a delicious trail snack.

1/2 cup beef jerky
1/2 cup cranberry leather
1/2 cup raisins

Later you can add:
1/4 cup chunky style peanut butter
1/4 cup dry (powdered) milk

Chop the jerky and cranberry leather into small pieces. Add the raisins. Place in a blender. Using the highest speed chop all ingredients together.

At this point, you may choose to place this into a Ziploc bag as is and serve in a warmed tortilla.

As an option, you can add 1/4 cup peanut butter and 1/4 cup powdered milk to the mixture. Stir until all the ingredients are combined.

Portion into once ounce servings and roll into balls. Let sit uncovered for 3 hours until dry to touch.
Store in airtight container.

These useful insulators are easy to make and help maintain the desired temperature.

Using closed cell pad:
1. Set your pot on the pad. Trace around the bottom of the pot. Add an 1/8 inch to the circle. Then cut this circle out of the pad.

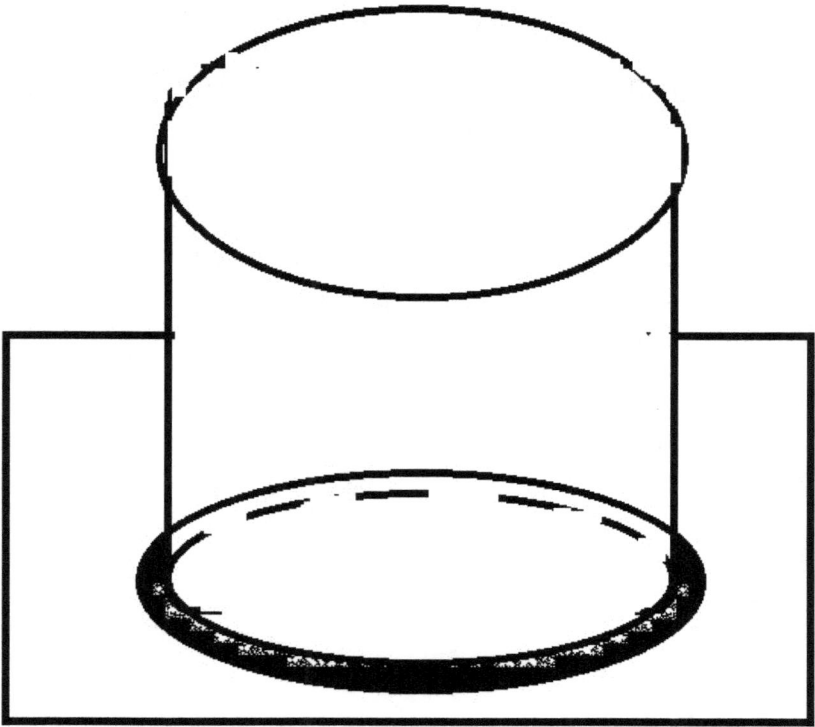

2. Measure the circumference (edge of the circle) that you just cut out, using a measuring tape or string. Add 1/4 inch to this length. This will be the length of the rectangle you need.

3. Measure the height of your pot with the lid on it. Add 1/2 inch to this. This will be the width of the rectangle.

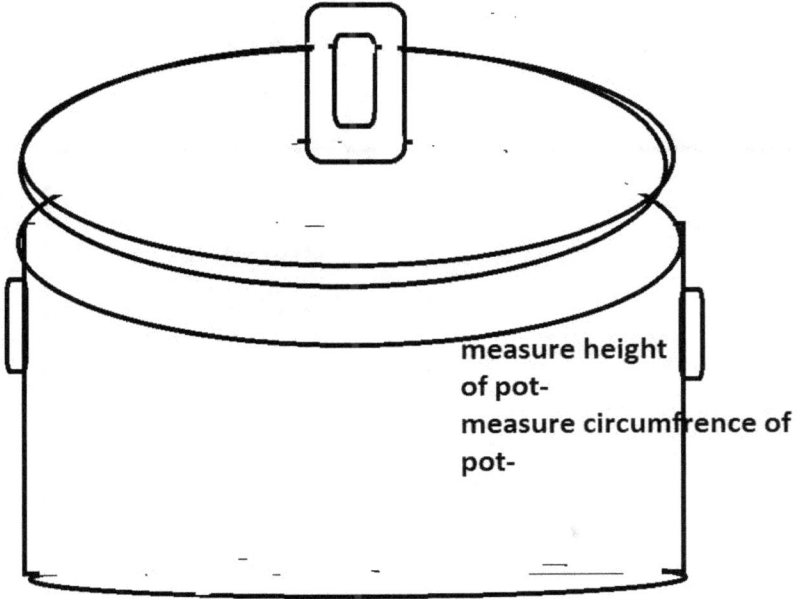

measure height of pot-
measure circumfrence of pot-

4. Take the two measurements obtained in numbers 2 and 3. Cut out a rectangle of those dimensions.

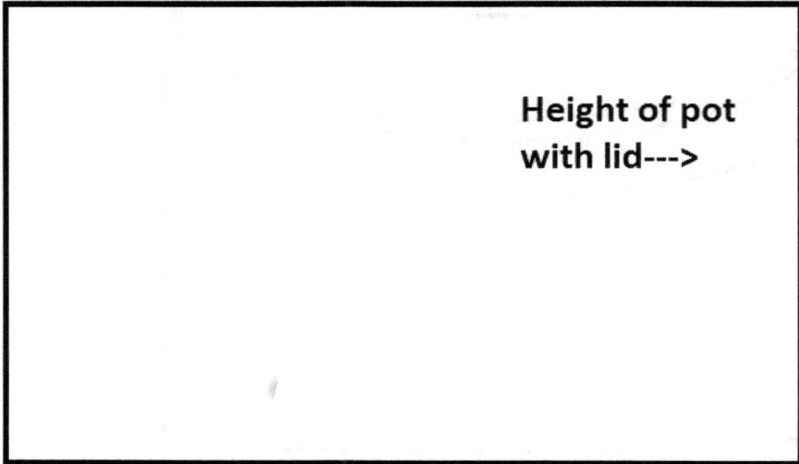

```
                                    Height of pot
                                    with lid--->
```

<--circumfrence of pot plus 1/2 inch-->

5. Using glue and duct tape, join the edges of the rectangle. You should have a cylinder.

6. Set this cylinder on the circle you cut out so that the bottom pad for the cozy fits neatly inside just at the bottom. Secure inside and out with duct tape, flanging inward over the bottom.

7. Set this cozy, bottom side up, on another piece of closed cell pad. Trace around it, to form the top of your cozy.

8. Cut this top circle out.

9. If you wish to add a handle, place one in the middle by cutting two parallel 1 inch slots in the top, 2 inches apart.

10. Thread a cord through slits and tie knot to secure.

Food List For 7 days in Garcia Bear Canister

I've heard all kinds of things about bear canisters. Until I actually bought one for the hike on the Continental Divide Trail, I really couldn't imagine fitting enough food and calories into it.

This is the Garcia Bear Canister. It weighs 2 pounds 11 ounces when empty. I used my GI trail can opener to slide the slots at the top when I needed to open it. You can also use a dime. It makes a nice trail table. It's somewhat slippery, so test how you plan to carry this in your pack.

Use this list with the accompanying specifications to plan a resupply. This is an actual week of food that I used for seven days.

Item-	Amount/ weight Meal	Grams of Protein	Calories	Notes
Instant coffee	2 ounces	0	0	One cup at breakfast One cup at supper
Pop tarts	14 ounces 4 double packages, 4 breakfasts	16	1,600	Be sure to buy the frosted ones.
Oatmeal	20 ounces 3 breakfasts/ 4 suppers	44	1,600	French Toast flavor, instant
M&Ms plain	34 ounces, for lunch gorp, use as filler in canister	48	5,040	This is a lot of chocolate, can substitute nuts. Take hiking style and digestion into account.
Raisons	15 ounce box, use for lunch GORP, can add to oatmeal	11	1,430	Too sticky to use as filler.
Peanuts	13 ounces, use for lunch GORP, or add to ramen supper for interest	78	1,950	Can use as filler, may leave salty residue
Pretzels	13 ounces, use for lunch GORP	39	1,560	Can add bits to soup as appetizer
Ramen	12 ounces (4 packages) 2 suppers	32	1,600	Creamy chicken flavors Can be eaten raw, or solar cooked

Self-Rising Corn meal	6.75 ounces 2 suppers	8	400	Make like a mush, can bring bacon bits to flavor, or parmesan cheese
Bouillon cubes	2.5 ounces, 6 cubes For suppers (or soup-flavoring)	12	180	Tomato flavor Knorr brand
Hard candy	9.5 ounces 49 pieces	0	882	Great for dry areas, sore throats 7 per day
Animal crackers	7 ounces - use for lunch GORP	14	840	Had the room, so I threw them in
Instant mashed potatoes	5.25 ounces	12	480	These can be added to thicken soup.
Totals	154 ounces 9.625 pounds food	314 grams of protein (44.85 per day) WHO recommends 40/adult	17,562 calories (2,508.85 per day)	This is 7 full days of food. It can be stretched to 9 by diluting and rationing, and fits into canister. Bring plastic bag for packing lunch each day. All packaging has been removed, and no garbage will accrue.

Variations can be made without increasing volume. For instance, Grits could be substituted for cornmeal, Snicker bars could be had

instead of Pop tarts. The items found here are very basic. I learned to use high calories "filler" instead of things like rice.

The Method

The first step, like any resupply, is to remove all excess packaging. Using high quality Ziploc bags repackage the oatmeal, raisons, ramen noodles etc.

I bring a couple empty quart Ziplocs so that every morning I can pack my "lunch" out of this mass of goodies. I carry my lunch in a Brawnygear belt loop pouch during the day. Any food not finished at lunch portion I eat at supper for dessert.
My bear canister came with a heavy plastic bag liner. This is a great way to keep all the filler clean, and hold down food smells. Keep and use this bag.

Place the pop tarts, still in their silver wrappers, but without the box, into the canister which is lined with a stout plastic bag.

Next, add the ziploc bags of oatmeal, grains, and raisons into canister , tucking them around the poptarts, making them conform to the sides of the canister. Bust up the ramen noodles to make a more condensed package.

Place each bag of food inside canister form tight layers pressing down to remove air pockets.

Once you have all the packaged food items in the canister, pour the peanuts and M&Ms into it, and shake so they fill in all the holes.
The grains make good trail items because they don't leave many gaps in the packing process. However, you'll find you can put a lot of calories in the canister loosely by using nuts and candies as filler, and following this method.

Unpacking for meals:
Have a clean bag ready so that as you look for the breakfast fixings, you can carefully scoop aside the Trail mix/peanuts and m&ms and lay on the plastic bag, or in your clean, dry, cooking pot.

Have an empty quart size ziploc bag available and use this time to ration out lunch. Carry your lunch outside the canister while you hike during the day.

As you repack the canister, plan what you'll need for supper, and be sure that it is near the top. Replace "filler". Lock securely. Test to be sure it won't open while you're hiking.

Keep meals simple and as the days go by you will find this process gets easier.
Be sure to lock the canister after each use so the lid doesn't pop off while hiking.

Rainmaker and I at Sonora Pass. He taught me the fine art of Yogi. Yogi Bear is the mascot for Yellowstone. Yogi is an expert at making friends. With his charming ways and casual conversation he is able to win over tourists loaded with picnic baskets who suddenly feel like sharing the bounty.

At first I felt guilty when invited to share a plate of food with a family enjoying a summer bar-b-que. But these kind strangers had more than they could eat, they promised me, and wouldn't I just like to sit a spell and tell them about my hike. Gradually I came to accept the fact that our crossing paths was good. I'd enjoy their generosity, they would take crazy wild true stories home with them, and share those stories around the water cooler.

THE BACKPACKER'S TRAIL KITCHEN

**This kit all nests together inside the pot except for the spoon.
From left to right: pot lid, pot support, folded windscreen. Setting on
top the blue ditty bag is the pot, a soda can stove, a plastic trail cup
with a spoon, a small baggie of salt, and a lighter.**

This kit weighs 8.5 five ounces and is very economical. The pot support is
made from a gutter guard I found at a hardware store. It can be expanded
or contracted to fit various size pots.

The plastic cup is from a health food cereal. The windscreen is made out of
oven liner.

Gone are the days of heavy backpacking cook sets. Years ago hikers would
bring several pots and pans, a stove which required priming and canister
fuel.

With the ¼ ounce soda can stove, various fuels can be found and used. I
discuss that in the next Chapter .

This is just another variation of a backpacking cook set. Notice the set fits into a plastic bowl with cup as the lid. The pot is a small aluminum can with a foil lid. The soda can stove has a beer can windscreen. The pot support is made from a tin can, and is beginning to show rust. This kit fits into a mesh ditty bag and weighs 3.5 ounces.

Using this ultralight set requires a little more planning. Food is simply rehydrated in the bowl with water heated to boiling in the can. A very fuel efficient method, I used this system on the last 500 miles of my successful through hike on the Appalachian Trail.

Foods which lend themselves to this approach are: instant potatoes, ramen noodles, instant rice, instant oatmeal, and instant soups. Items which require more cooking do not work with this system. Spaghetti, dehydrated stews and scalloped potatoes will not rehydrate enough to be easily digested, so I save them for another hike.

By using the hot water to rehydrate foods in the plastic containers, and reheating additional water, meals are easy to clean up and volume depends solely on how much water you want to heat. Be sure to have a safe way of removing pot from heat source.

Bread fills out the meal, along with beverages like coffee and hot cocoa.

A coffee can and lid make a cheap pot into which you can nest a drinking cup, stove and windscreen. This system can utilize gutter nail stakes as the pot support. A regular spoon completes the set.

By being creative, you can save a lot of money on your cook set. The plastic lid serves as a clean spoon holder and seals the coffee can. I especially liked using this can when making Cowboy coffee because the rim held back the grounds while I poured steaming coffee into my trail cup.

In this photo we see from left to right:
Homemade fuel tablets, two types of spoons, a ditty bag for the water purification Chlorine bottle, and a cotton bandana.

Only use the cotton bandana as a pot holder if it's dry. Wet bandanas will create steam and may burn you badly. I use my trail gloves because they are nearly always dry and fit well.

A tip: don't cut your spoon down so that it nests in your pot. Murphy's Law of Trail Spoons says that any spoon which can fit in your pot, will. The spoon will fall into your pot, especially when it's full of oatmeal or chicken Alfredo. It will end up submerged in the hot food and digging it out of there is very messy.

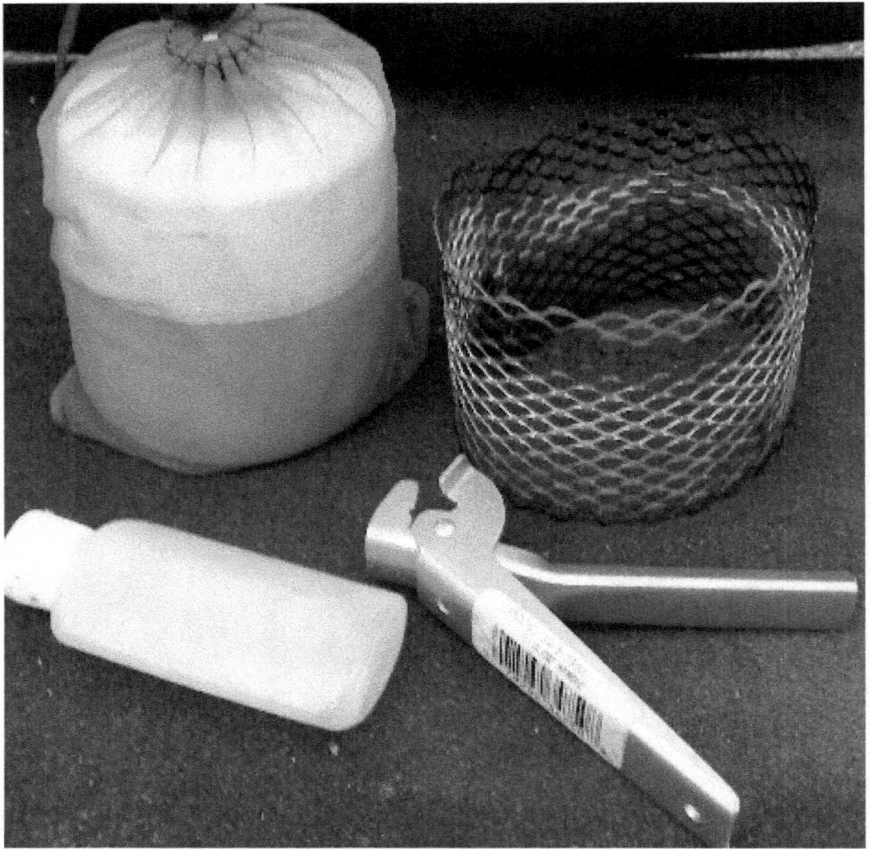

Shown here is the nesting Ultralight Cook Set in a mesh bag. Then, there is a closer view of an all-purpose pot support and in the front row, a bottle squirt bottle filled with canola oil and a pot lifter.

The tight Ultralight Three ounce system nestles well with little extra space. Every component has a purpose.

The all-purpose pot support is rust free, easy to make, and can be nested into any system because you make it yourself. Be sure to file any sharp edges.

Bottles for liquid are obtained easily. If you're recycling, choose a bottle that had liquid in it when you first bought it. I usually keep things like this in its own plastic baggie, just in case it decides to leak anyways.

The pot lifter is totally optional. My hiking partner, Rainmaker, always had one. I use mittens or gloves. Some will use a bandana. You do need something for lifting the pot while it's hot, or lifting the lid to check progress.

The water purification process is necessary in most cases. I recycle soda bottles for trail use. They are strong, come in various sizes, have small or wide mouth openings, and are easily replaced. Add a bottle or remove one from your total system as trails require.

I usually wrap electrical tape around my water bottles to aid in handling and for emergencies. Plus, they are easily identified when hikers gather around a picnic table.

This platypus water container holds two quarts and takes up little space. It holds my camp water, although I had friends on the Pacific Crest Trail who carried several and placed them in their packs full. Be prepared to fix them if they start to leak, however. Carry several bottles when backpacking, in case one starts to leak. You don't want all your water in just one container heading through the desert.

The platypus disaster I remember most vividly happened on the Appalachian Trail.
One night I heard a loud splash while sleeping on the top platform in a crowded shelter in the Smoky Mountain National Park. It was early spring and cold. I thought it had started raining during the night and someone had camped and was shaking the water off their tarp.

The next morning, as we thu-hikers began packing up to continue up the Appalachian Trail, a guy yelled out, "What happened to my platypus?"
He showed us this gallon sized water container with a huge hole in it.
During the night a bear had come to check out the fence and saw the water bag. I heard the loud splash when he took his bite.
It was funny for us, but not for this dude who had spent good money on his gear.

I tested this ice scraper as a pancake turner. It's lightweight, not totally ideal, but good enough.

On overnight backpacking trips, I'll sometimes carry an insulated mug, a secondary pan, an extra stove or a 48 ounce coffee can exclusively for making cowboy coffee.
With a good basic cook set, you can add luxuries on occasion without much increase in weight or bulk.

Simple cook sets allow people to try backpacking without a huge investment. One hiker left his titanium cup five miles back near a creek. He was not about to back track for it even though it was very expensive. With the sets shown here there are few regrets. Next time you go to the grocery store, you can cruise the aisles looking for suitable replacements. Sometimes an ultralighter will buy the grocery item for the container more than the food inside.

Shown here are gallon sized Ziploc bags, a sandwich bag, and two tiny resealable bags one with salt, one with pills. Also shown is a plastic bottle with a favorite spice mix.

We also use the longer plastic resealable bags for various condiments and thickeners. A few bouillon cubes come in handy for Desperation Soup.

The water sack is a great way to have a lot of water available in camp yet take up little room in your pack. Before purchasing, check weight and capacity. Hang it in the sun to warm the water and save fuel while cooking.

While on the Colorado Trail, the maintainer's crew invited me to use their solar shower. The concept was the same as the water sack.
While full and laying in the sun all day, it warmed the water to a luscious 120 degrees. Then it was hoisted above the bather who then had a decent stream of five gallons of water. Below you see it used at a hand-washing station, surrounded by snow, at 11,500 feet.

SPECIAL TRICKS FOR THE ULTRALIGHTER

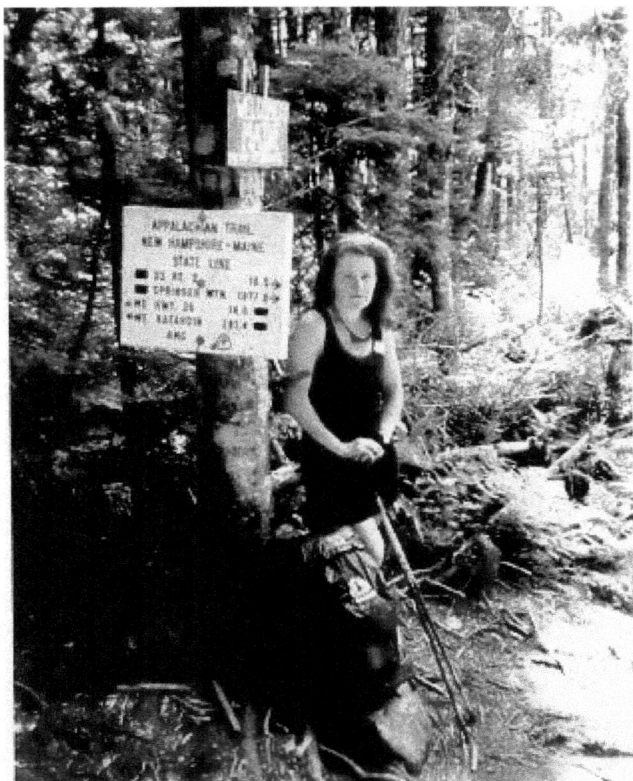

Crossing into Maine on the Appalachian Trail
I used this photo for my first book: My Journey to Freedom and Ultralight Backpacking. My 9 ounce silnylon backpack became one of my signature pieces which I designed and sewed myself. It lasted the entire trail. My base weight was just over 8 pounds.

My second book in this series is called **An Ultralighter's True Trail Stories—Beyond the Journey.**

I've studied and written about Ultralight backpacking for many years. My home page is hosted at **http://trailquest.net/BRindex.html.**

It has many of my discoveries plus strategies. I maintain two blogs, http://brawnyview.blogspot.com and http://thefemalesurvivalist.blogspot.com.
You can read more there about my latest adventures and discoveries.

Water can become the single heaviest item, so I developed certain techniques for staying hydrated. Dehydration can cause indigestion, constipation, and lead to heat stroke in the desert. It will also cause a reduction in blood volume , which can make you sleep colder at night.

I've developed some strategies to staying hydrated while minimalizing the weight.
In well watered areas you can carry two water bottles, each with a capacity of 24 ounces. Drink one as soon as purification is complete. The other one you keep full until another water source is located.
When you arrive at the next water source, drink the reserved bottle. Refill both bottles and treat them with your purification chemicals.

Continue hiking, and when the first bottle is ready, drink it, and save the next one until you arrive at water again. This way a person stays well hydrated without running out of water.

In the desert this strategy changes. Compute the miles to the next sure water and divide the amount of water carried among the hours necessary to reach that source. The most I ever carried, even while traversing the Mojave Desert was 5 liters of water.

Try to get started at daybreak, while it is still cool. Then during the heat of the day rest in the shade, preferably at a water source. You may have to create your own shade but hopefully there will be a rock overhang or Joshua tree.
Cook and wash the dishes, brush your teeth, and wash your body at a water source if possible. If there is still a lot of daylight when that source is reached, take care of these necessities and hike until dark.

Whenever you reach water, drink as much as you can hold, resting and waiting for a while so the body can absorb the moisture. Then drink as much as you can hold before moving on. This method will get you through a lot of desert miles on a daily basis.

Some people will night hike to avoid the heat of desert hiking, thus decreasing the quantity of water carried.

One small warning, though. Remember that snakes hunt at night, and that a trail which is not well marked may become confusing, if not lost. Also, if your night light fails, you may not have a decent place to stop to rest until daylight.
A full moon on a clear night may provide enough light to enjoy night hiking on a well maintained trail, if that's your passion, but it is not something you should plan on doing as a regular coping method.

The food bag is another potentially massive load.
I try to keep my food weight to just over one pound per day. This is very minimal for most people. Most men need twice that figure. A 160-pound man whose goal is to carry 15% of his body weight would have 24 pounds pack weight to work with. That goal can be maintained by the dedicated ultralighter, still allowing for additional food weight.

It's very important to learn to ration your food, even if you're really hungry. Be sure you have enough so that you can eat every day you are hiking. This concept may seem obvious, but I've met people who ended up with no food and an entire day of hiking until the next town could be reached. They became faint, and had to "borrow" supplies.

Foods which are heavy and bulky but satisfying on the trail are bagels, whole wheat bread, cheese, and summer sausage. I splurge on these during short resupplies. By occasionally switching to whole foods, you can fulfill any cravings you have. Sometimes you might order a whole 20 inch pizza in town, knowing you'll never finish it. Pack it out for supper that evening.

When resupplying for long distances, however, I used high density foods, which are compact, filling, and usually require water for meal preparation.

I've recently developed a Slow Burning Soda Can stove. It's easy to make right on the trail and only weighs 3/8 ounce (12 grams). With this stove, a person can carry biscuit mix, pancake mix, and even cake mixes and bake right in camp. These powders have a good weight to calorie ratio.

You can make this stove yourself using just one soda can, a jackknife and tape.

Here is a Pizza I made using a slow burning stove.

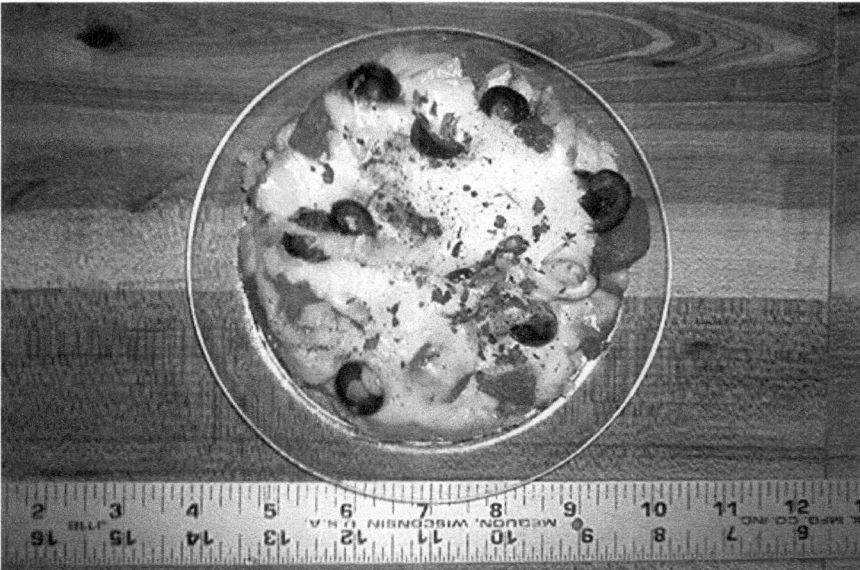

Practice using a slow burning stove so you too can make breads, cakes and even the pizza pictured above.

Here are just a few of the recipes I've made using this process. A snuffer is typically a metal lid or similar item that will extinguish the flame by suffocating the air supply.

OATMEAL MUFFIN

When you are tired of hauling that instant oatmeal around, make a delicious muffin for breakfast!

Place one ounce of fuel into your soda can stove. Place pot support and windscreen around it. Use a simmer attachment, if you have one. If using the slow burner stove, make sure the flame is going before continuing.

Prepare the muffin batter by stirring together:
1/2 cup any cake mix
1 ounce package of flavored instant oatmeal
1/4 cup water

This should make stiff dough.
Light stove. Wait until just a small flame appears. Place 1 tablespoon of oil into pot and spoon mixture into it. Then set pot on pot support.

Cook for 10 - 12 minutes covered. Top of lid should become hot to touch. The less peeking you do, the sooner it will be done.

Remove lid with gloves, and if the muffin is firm but moist, it is done. If not, cover and allow to cook a while longer.

When muffin is done, remove pot from heat. Using a snuffer, put out the stove.
Allow to cool before removing from pan.

For variations, add chopped nuts, raisins, or fruit to the muffin batter before cooking.

Now we are getting beyond typical trail food with a gourmet dish like Quiche.

Crust:
1/2-cup self-rising flour
3 tablespoons oil

Mix flour and oil well. Pat into pot, spreading thinly and up the sides to form a bowl to hold the egg mixture.

Quiche:
1/2 cup powdered eggs
2 tablespoons powdered cheese
1/2-cup water (warm is better because it will speed cooking)
1 tablespoon parsley
1/4 teaspoon each, garlic, and pepper
Salt to taste

Mix the powders, water and spices together. Spoon into prepared crust. You can add vegetables by first soaking dehydrated vegetables for an hour or using fresh chopped vegetables. Drain all excess water from vegetables. Add to the egg mixture.

Prepare stove by placing one ounce of fuel into your stove, with pot support, and windscreen surrounding it. Light the stove and wait for small flame to appear. Set the pot on the pot support, cover with lid.

Allow to cook for about 15 minutes. Lift the lid using potholder or other utensil, and check the progress of your quiche. It is ready if the egg mixture is firm. If it is still soupy, replace lid and allow to cook a while longer.

When your quiche firm, it is done. This is an amazing trail dish. I like mine with catsup. It isn't advised to remove from pot before eating because the crust may crumble excessively. Eat straight from the pot.

I never would have thought a regular cake mix, without the eggs and oil would work as a delicious trail treat. It's fantastic. When on the trail, you can now have cake on your birthday. Limit the candles to how many you are willing to haul out of town.

Place one ounce of fuel into your soda can stove. Set pot support and windscreen around it.

Prepare the cake mix by stirring together:
1/2 cup any cake mix
1/4 cup water

This should make stiff dough.
Light stove. Wait for small flame.

Put one tablespoon oil into pot and spoon mixture into it. Then set pot on pot support.
Cook for 10 - 12 minutes covered. Top of lid should become hot to touch.

Remove lid with gloves, and if the cake is firm but moist it is done. If not, cover and allow to cook a while longer.

When cake is done, remove pot from heat. Using the snuffer, put out the stove.
Allow to cool before removing from pan.

Prepare frosting from 1 cup powdered sugar.
For flavoring add 1 teaspoon cocoa powder or 1 teaspoon powdered drink mix
1 tablespoon milk, or water.
Spread frosting over cake.

Dust with sprinkles if you have them. Place candle on top. Light and make your wishes!

Ann C. from Zephyr Hills, Florida, requested this recipe. It was made in my 2-pint pot, but can be expanded to fill a larger one. A big thanks to Ann for her great suggestion.

To dehydrate chili, you can buy canned chili, and spread thinly on a sauce type dehydrator sheet. Use medium setting, and allow to dry until crumbly in your hand. If there is meat in the mixture, be sure to towel off any excess fat, which will not dehydrate. Place dehydrated chili in a Ziploc bag.

You may make your own favorite chili recipe, and dehydrate according to the above suggestions.

You will need enough **rehydrated chili** to fill pot half way and the cornbread batter, recipe below.

Cornbread batter:
1/2 cup self-rising cornmeal
3 tablespoons water
1 tablespoon oil

Mix the cornmeal and the water. It should make stiff dough. Set aside. Pour one tablespoon of oil into your pot. Prepare stove.

Place one and a half ounce of fuel into your stove, with pot support, and windscreen surrounding it. Light the stove and wait for the tiny flame. Fill your pot half full with chili. Set the pot on the pot support, cover with lid.

Allow the chili to heat thoroughly, stirring to prevent burning on bottom.

When chili is boiling, pour cornbread mixture into the pot, spreading it to cover the chili. Cover with lid. Allow to cook for about 5 - 7 more minutes. Lift the lid using potholder or other utensil, and check the progress of your cornbread. It is ready if the dough is firm but moist. If it is still sticky, replace lid and allow to cook a while longer.

When your cornbread is firm, it is done. This is a fabulously filling meal. Served with a slice of cheese, this meal is heaven.

FRESH BISCUIT

This recipe answers the craving for hot bread on the trail.

1/2 - cup biscuit mix (use the kind that only requires milk or water)
1/4 - cup water

Stir the mix and water together to form stiff dough. Set aside.

Pour approximately 1 ounce of fuel into your soda can stove. Place the pot support and windscreen around it. Light the fuel with a match.

Into your pot place 1 tablespoon oil and the dough. Set your pot on the pot support. Place the lid on immediately.

If you are having problems with burning on the bottom, perhaps your pot is very thin. In this case I recommend spooning the dough into the pot before setting on the pot support. Be sure the flame is closed down as far as possible without extinguishing.

John Austin of Corinna, Maine said that after burning the bottom of his biscuits a few times, he put a peanut butter jar metal cap between the bottom of the pot and the biscuits. This allowed for a 3/8" air space for the heat to dissipate into the pot. He stated that when he used the jar cap, his biscuits came out golden brown with no burns.

As the bread cooks, the top of the lid will become hot. This is simulating a slow cooking oven. Inside, the biscuit will rise and begin cooking from the bottom up. After about 4 minutes, rotate the pot about 90 degrees, to help the bottom cook evenly without burning.

The top of the lid should be getting quite hot to the touch. Always move the pot with some type of hand protection to avoid burns.

After about 10 minutes, remove the lid. If the bread is done, it will be dry to the touch. Use your spoon to test for doneness.
If it is not done, cover, and cook for a few more minutes.

When the top of the biscuit is done and dry to the touch, remove from heat. Take the lid off your pot and allow to cool for a few minutes. It should come out of the pot easily.

Here is a complete meal. The dumplings thicken the broth, turning it into gravy consistency.

1 -cup water
1 chicken bouillon cube
1 tablespoon minced onions
dash of garlic
chicken (canned or dehydrated)

Place one ounce of fuel into your soda can stove. Set pot support and windscreen around it.

Put the water, bouillon cube, onions, garlic and chicken in the pot. Light the stove, and place covered pot on heat.

Prepare dumpling mix:
3/4 cup biscuit mix
dash of sage
1/4 - cup water
This should make stiff dough. Uncover pot, spoon onto hot chicken mixture. Recover.
Cook for 10-12 minutes covered. Top of lid should become hot to touch.

Remove lid with gloves, and if the biscuit is firm but moist it is done. If not, cover and allow to cook a while longer.

When biscuit is done, remove pot from heat.

This is a very satisfying meal.

Any fruit may be used for this trail dessert. Take advantage of fresh berries along the trail, too.

One medium apple, washed
3/4 - cup water
1/3 - cup brown or white sugar
1/4 - teaspoon cinnamon
Dash of salt

Biscuit Topping:
2/3 cup biscuit mix
1/4 scant cup water
1 - tablespoon sugar

Mix the powdered mix with the water. It should make stiff dough. Set aside.

Thinly slice apple into your pot. Add the water, sugar, spice and salt. Other spices, which taste good with trail fruits, are nutmeg, cloves or ginger. Cover pot and prepare stove.

Place one ounce of fuel into your stove, with pot support, and windscreen surrounding it. Light the stove and set the covered pot on it.

Allow the fruit mixture to come to a boil.

Pour prepared biscuit mixture over hot fruit mixture and cover with lid.

Cook for 10 more minutes. Lift the lid using potholder or other utensil, and check the progress of your cobbler. It is ready if the dough is firm but moist. If it is still sticky, replace lid and allow to cook a while longer.

Eat dessert directly from the pot. Best served alongside a fresh cup of coffee.

PIZZA

This pizza is a vegetarian supreme. It was made in a 2 pint pot, but can be expanded to fill a larger one. Toppings are limited only by your imagination.

Toppings For Pizza In Photo:
chopped onions
sliced olives
3/4 - cup diced tomatoes
1/3 - cup mozzarella cheese, grated, or broken into small bits
1 tablespoon Parmesan cheese
Dash of salt, pepper, basil

Pizza Dough:
1/2 cup biscuit mix
3 tablespoons water
1/4 teaspoons garlic and oregano
1 tablespoon oil

Mix the powdered mix with the water. It should make stiff dough. Set aside. Pour one tablespoon of oil into your pot. Prepare stove.

Place one ounce of fuel into your stove, with pot support, and windscreen surrounding it. Light the stove and wait for the flame.

Pour prepared biscuit mixture into the pot, spreading it to cover the entire bottom.
Set the pot on pot support. Cover with lid. Place pot back on heat and allow to cook for 7 more minutes.
Lift the lid using potholder or other utensil, and check the progress of the pizza crust. It is ready if the dough is firm but moist. If it is still sticky, replace lid and allow to cook a while longer.

When the crust is firm, spoon the tomatoes, vegetables, and cheeses over it. Replace the lid and allow to cook until the cheese is melted.

Sprinkle salt, pepper and basil over entire pizza.

Place one ounce of fuel into your soda can stove. Set pot support and windscreen around it.

Prepare the coffee cake mix by stirring together:
3/4 cup biscuit mix
3 tablespoons sugar
1/4 - cup water
1/4 - cup raisins
1/2 - teaspoon cinnamon

This should make stiff dough.

Light stove. Put a teaspoon of oil into your pot.
Once the flame is going, set pot on pot support and spoon mixture into it.

Cook for 10 - 12 minutes covered. Top of lid should become hot too touch. Remove lid with gloves and if the cake is firm but moist it is done. If not, cover and allow to cook a while longer.

When cake is done, remove pot from heat.
Allow to cool before removing from pan.

Prepare frosting from:
1/2 cup powdered sugar
1 - teaspoon vanilla, or milk, or water.

Spread frosting over cake.
This is a very tasty treat.

Basics Ultralighter Secrets

When you arrive in town, eat well and often. Eat the stuff you're craving. Many hikers crave ice cream, which is full of calcium, protein and fats. Once you recognize your hiking style, resupplying will become second nature.

Some hikers will cook breakfast every morning without fail. For others, cleaning the pot just isn't worth the trouble, preferring an extra half hour of sleep and a Pop-tart or Snickers as they pack up for the day. There are hikers who will stop and cook during the day. Then, in camp at day's end, some make coffee upon arriving, others holding off until they cook supper just before bed.

Often, I'll prepare a snack bag and carry it on my belt. If I want to do a twenty to thirty mile day, I slow down while eating, but just keep going until I arrive at the destination. You can trail your body to do this over time.

If you have a hiking partners check out their style. You may adapt and cook together, or develop a separate cooking system. Rainmaker and I always cooked separately and in camp. We carried our own stoves and pots, our own water and food supplies. We both use the soda can stove, which will nest in any pot. It is the weight of the fuel that is the consideration.

FUELS FOR THE SODA CAN STOVE

I've used a soda can stove for all my backpacking adventures since 2001. During that time, I've burned many types of fuel because not all trail towns have denatured alcohol, the first choice and most efficient stove fuel.

Never attempt to burn Coleman fuel or any gasoline based fuel in a soda can stove. It will blow up.

Second choice of fuel is HEET, a gasoline additive. This fuel can usually be found at gas stations, Wal-Mart, or other convenience stores.

Barring that, **90% rubbing alcohol** is good. Usually you will find a **70% rubbing alcohol**. It works, but the lower percentage means there's more water, and it's harder to light.

In cold weather, or above 9,000 feet elevation, you may need to apply heat via cigarette lighter, to the outside bottom of the stove to warm up the aluminum stove which helps it light. Warming the fuel helps at high elevations. Do this by placing the fuel bottle inside your shirt, next to your body heat, or pouring a little in the stove, then holding the stove with your thumb and index finger, apply heat via cigarette lighter for a minute or so.

Only use liquid fuels **inside** the soda can stove.

If you need or want to use solid fuels, flip the stove over and use the concave section for Esbit or Hexamine tablets. You can ship these in the mail to towns along the trail. Buy Esbit at Campmor.com. Sometimes Wal-Mart will carry the 24 pack of Hexamine tablets. You can find fuel tablets at Amazon.com also.

While hiking on the Colorado Trail, I had to use Coghlans Camp Fuel Sticks. They were somewhat sooty, but I was able to cook 12 meals with one package.

Burn solid fuels on the flip side of the Soda Can Stove.

Make your own fuel sticks by filling an ice cube tray with dry wood shavings, sawdust, or 100% cotton balls. Melt wax over this and allow to cool. Remove from the tray. You will have nice little blocks of fuel.

You can burn these solid fuel tablets in a clean tuna fish can as well. No need to buy a special stove if you're going to play with this concept.

This photo shows a candle being melted directly over a tray of wood chips. This is an easy and efficient way to create your own fuel cubes.

One of my all-time favorite backpacking foods is Oatmeal.

100 % Whole Grain Oats must be one of the best all-around foods. A 42 ounce container costs is inexpensive, has 30 servings, each one consisting of 1/2 cup dry oats. In this serving there are 150 calories, 5 grams of **protein**, and 4 grams of fiber.

I use oatmeal as a staple in my backpacking food bag. It can be eaten raw or cooked. An easy way to fix it without cooking in a pot is to simply add one and a fourth cup (1 1/4 cup) of boiling water to a bowl which has half a cup of dry oatmeal in it. Stir just enough to mix.

Cover this bowl with a plate or lid, and let set until the oatmeal has absorbed most of the water. Season with salt, sugar and **cinnamon**. For an extra caloric and nutritional boost, add one tablespoon canola oil, chopped nuts and/or **raisins**.

Oatmeal can be carried for a long time without spoilage as long as it is kept dry. When I eat oatmeal raw as a survival snack, I also drink a lot of water to aid in digestion.

This is an easy food item which can be found in many **convenience** stores along the trail, easily packed into a bear canister and requires little or no fuel for preparation.

MAKING THE ULTRALIGHT FOOD BAG LAST

I've found some discussions on Ultralighter vs. Minimalism with the survival theory in mind. It's amazing how misunderstood the true Ultralighter is.

And I'm also surprised how often the necessary skill-building and trail-tested period is overlooked. Building skills as an ultralight backpacker is a journey. Don't expect to just arrive because of reading. You arrive by doing.

I hiked with a guy on the Appalachian Trail for a while up in New Hampshire. The mere fact we were running across trail magic in the form of serious food stashes, bright colorful coolers set out along the trail for thru hikers, and handouts while crossing the road should not have made such an impact on him. Any of these supplements to our food bags could end at any time. Yet, he sort of got used to it and started carrying way too little food. He resupplied in Gorham, and what he bought ran out two days early.

Now, when I see my food stash getting low, I either pile on the miles, or do half rations. Our body can live off fat stored inside, but our minds need to know all is well and we are in control. Hence a meal, no matter how skimpy or how thin the oatmeal, needs to happen on a regular basis.

Blood sugar levels are kept within limits with smaller, rather than no calorie, installations.
I found out this guy had run out of food when I witnessed him acting dizzy and nearly falling over. I asked him, "What's up?"

He admitted he had run out of food, but said not to worry, he'd been in the Special Forces back in his youth, a long time ago, and claimed he knew how to hike on nothing for 20 miles.

Rabun County was dry on Sundays. But this sketch reminds me that a little preplanning goes a long ways.

As I watched my temporary hiking partner's face explain all this, I realized I had just enough to spare. I wasn't letting him off the hook, either, and made him promise to buy me lunch. We headed, hiking faster, getting into town hungrier and much earlier the next morning.
Better believe he bought me lunch.

Moral of the story, when estimating food needs for a section of trail, plan regular mileage days and enough calories. If things go bad and it's taking longer, stretch the food by doing 3/4 rations earlier, rather than later. Use water to thin out the soup and the oatmeal. Eat only half a candy bar.
A real ultra-lighter never needs bailing out.
Sometimes we take that gift of a Snicker's bar, but its gravy, not life or death.

Out of clutter, find Simplicity.
From discord, find Harmony.
In the middle of difficulty lies Opportunity.

ALBERT EINSTEIN's Three Rules of Work

Vital Statistics

---per 1/4 cup serving:
Calories:130
Total Fat: Zero
Cholesterol: Zero
Carbohydrates: 31 grams
Dietary Fiber: 2 grams
Protein: 1 gram
Iron : 6% daily requirements
Calcium: 2 % daily requirements

I love raisins. Just for fun, I've added some of my recipes for enjoying these morsels of delight.

Fantastic Fruit
1 cup raisins
1 cup prunes
Place raisins and prunes in a saucepan. Cover with water and simmer together for twenty minutes. Can be eaten like this or blend until pureed to use as sauce.

Proven very effective for keeping the bowels moving.

Stewed Raisins

1 cup raisins
1/4 teaspoon of cinnamon
dash of nutmeg
dash of salt
Whipped Cream

Place raisins, spices and salt in a saucepan. Cover with water. Bring to boil, then cut back the heat, and allow to simmer until the raisins are plump, about 15 minutes. Serve while still warm, with whipped cream.

Hot Cocoa with Raisins
--*Here is a variation that raisin lovers will appreciate.*

Put 1/4 cup raisins in a mug. Fill mug with water, microwave for 2 minutes, or until hot. Add your favorite instant hot cocoa mix. Stir well. As you sip the chocolate, the raisins will continue to soften and add sweetness. Eat raisins.

Raisin Trail Mix

1 cup raisins
1 cup nuts
1 cup chocolate chips
1 cup honey oats cereal

In a large Ziploc bag, combine all four ingredients. Shake well to mix. If it gets hot, the chocolate will melt, but once cool it will solidify into great trail chunks.

Ants on a Log

Fresh, raw celery, washed and cut into 3 inch lengths
creamy style peanut butter
raisins

Prepare celery sticks by washing then patting dry. Spread the creamy peanut butter on the celery. Lay raisins along the peanut butter, pressing into secure.

Brawny's Raisin Custard Meringue Pie

Pie Crust:
1 stick of margarine
1 cup flour

Melt margarine in saucepan and stir in flour. Press dough into a 10 inch pie plate. Prick with a fork in key locations.
Bake at 400 degrees, approximately 10 minutes until golden brown.
Remove from oven.

Filling:
2 tablespoons butter
1/4 cup flour
1/2 box raisons (about 8 ounces)
2 cups water
3/4 cups brown sugar
1/2 teaspoons cloves
3 egg yolks, slightly beaten
1/4 cup water

Melt butter, stir in flour. Add raisins, water and sugar. Simmer until raisins are soft and mixture begins to thicken. Stir eggs into the 1/4 cup water. Add to raisin mixture. Cook until thickened, about 3 minutes. Pour into prepared pie shell.

Meringue
To save time, you can top the pie with whipped cream instead.

With the 3 egg whites, prepare a meringue by whipping egg whites until frothy. Add bit by bit, 3 teaspoons white sugar. When it forms peaks, load onto pie filling. Bake at 375 until lightly browned. Remove from oven.

Allow to cool before devouring.

Carrot Raisin Slaw

2 cups grated carrots
1 cup raisins
1/2 cup lite mayonnaise
milk to moisten

Combine grated carrots, raisins, mayonnaise and milk in a nice glass bowl. Mix well and chill before serving.

Apple-Raisin Crisp

3 pounds fresh apples, peeled and sliced
1 cup raisins
3 Tablespoons flour
1 teaspoon cinnamon
1/4 teaspoon nutmeg
dash of salt
topping, recipe below

Mix flour, cinnamon, nutmeg and salt together in large bowl. Stir well; add the sliced peeled apples and raisins. Pour the mixture into a 9x13 pan.

Make the topping below. Sprinkle over the apples. Bake at 350 degrees for 45 minutes until apples are bubbling and top is lightly browned. Great served with ice cream.

Crisp Topping

1 stick of softened margarine
1/2 cup white sugar
1/2 cup brown sugar
1 cup white flour
1 cup quick cooking oats

Blend the margarine and sugars together. Stir in the flour and oats. Spread over the above apple recipe. Bake as directed.

Cinnamon Raisin Sweet Rolls

1 1/4 cup warm water
1 tablespoon yeast
1 tablespoon sugar
3 tablespoons margarine
1 1/2 teaspoons salt
3 1/2 cups flour

In a medium sized bowl, dissolve yeast in water. Stir in the sugar, margarine, salt and 3 cups of flour.
Allow batter to rest for 10 minutes.

Using last 1/2 cups flour, knead for 5 minutes, and then roll out dough to a 14 x 18 inch rectangle.

Spread dough with:

2 tablespoons margarine
1/4 cup sugar and cinnamon mixture
1 cup of raisins, evenly over all.

Roll up length wise. Slice into 1/2 inch pieces, laying them down on a greased cookie sheet.
Allow dough to double in size before baking at 375 degrees for 10 minutes or until lightly browned.

Glaze:

Mix 2 cups powdered sugar with 1 teaspoon vanilla. Add 2 tablespoons milk, mix well. Spread over rolls just as they come from the oven.

Raisin Waldrof Salad

4 cups chopped apples
1 cup raisins
1/3 cup diced celery
1/4 cup white sugar
1/2 cup mayonnaise
milk to moisten

Combine apples, raisins, celery, sugar and mayonnaise and milk in a nice glass bowl. Blend together well. Chill before serving.

Raisin Chocolate Chews
Melting chocolate, either dark or almond
raisins

Melt chocolate in bowl, in the microwave, or in a saucepan slowly over low heat. Stir in raisins, coating well. Drop by teaspoons onto wax paper. Allow to set until firm.

Raisin Cabbage Slaw
2 cups shredded cabbage
1 cup raisins
1/2 cup salad dressing or mayonnaise
2 Tablespoons sugar
dash of salt

Combine cabbage, raisins, mayonnaise and milk in a bowl. Mix well. Chill.

Crossing the Kennebec in the Blazed Canoe-a designated method on the Appalachian Trail in Maine.

Never Die Alone

INDEX

135

...Soy Nut Trail Mix -19
...Maple Chex Mix -18

Breads-56
Apple Pancakes-62
Bagels (homemade)-60
...Chocolate Chip
....Cinnamon Raisin
...Nuts and Such
...Onion
...Rye
...Whole Wheat
Bear Sign (chocolate drop doughnuts)-59
Focaccia -65
Indian Fried Bread-58
Quick Yeast Muffins -64
Roasted Fresh Bread -64
Sweet Biscuits (bannock)-59
Tortillas -56
...Whole Wheat-57
...Authentic Mexican tortillas-57
Whole Wheat Rolls-63
Wild Berry Pancakes -63

Breakfasts-24
Breakfast Bars-26
Breakfast Burrito-32
Cornmeal Magic -29
Cream of Wheat -31
Favorite Camp Latte-26
Glorified Rice Chex (Cold Cereal)-27
Granola-28
Grits-29
Malted Breakfast Shake-26
Monster Mash with Nuts -31
Oatmeal and Raisins -30
Oatmeal with Peaches and Cream-30
Oatmeal with an Attitude-31
Power start Bars -27

Dehydrating-75

Non-Fiction

My Journey To Freedom and Ultralight Backpacking

An Ultralighter's True Trail Stories-Beyond The Journey

Wild Neighbors-a Children's Book

My First Cookbook-a Children's Interactive Book

The Cookbook Project-Sharing the Best

Fiction- C.J. Wellman

The River Survival Series-An EOTWAWKI

An End of Days- Book One

All Hell Won't Wait- Book Two

When Hell Comes Knocking-Book Three

No Storm Like This-Book Four

Delivered-Book Five

Primal Cuts-a horror story centered around the Ghost of Lake Yellowstone Hotel, Yellowstone National Park, WY.

Fatal Loves- sequel to Primal Cuts

This culinary guide for backpackers is filled with tips and recipes. It covers everything from the ultralight resupply in trail towns to dehydrating your own food, baking bread and packing a bear canister. Included are whimsical sketches and trail photos, adding a behind the scenes flavor to the second edition of this book.

www.ingramcontent.com/pod-product-compliance
Lightning Source LLC
Chambersburg PA
CBHW060510030426
42337CB00015B/1829

* 9 7 8 0 9 7 2 8 1 5 4 3 7 *